continued overleaf...

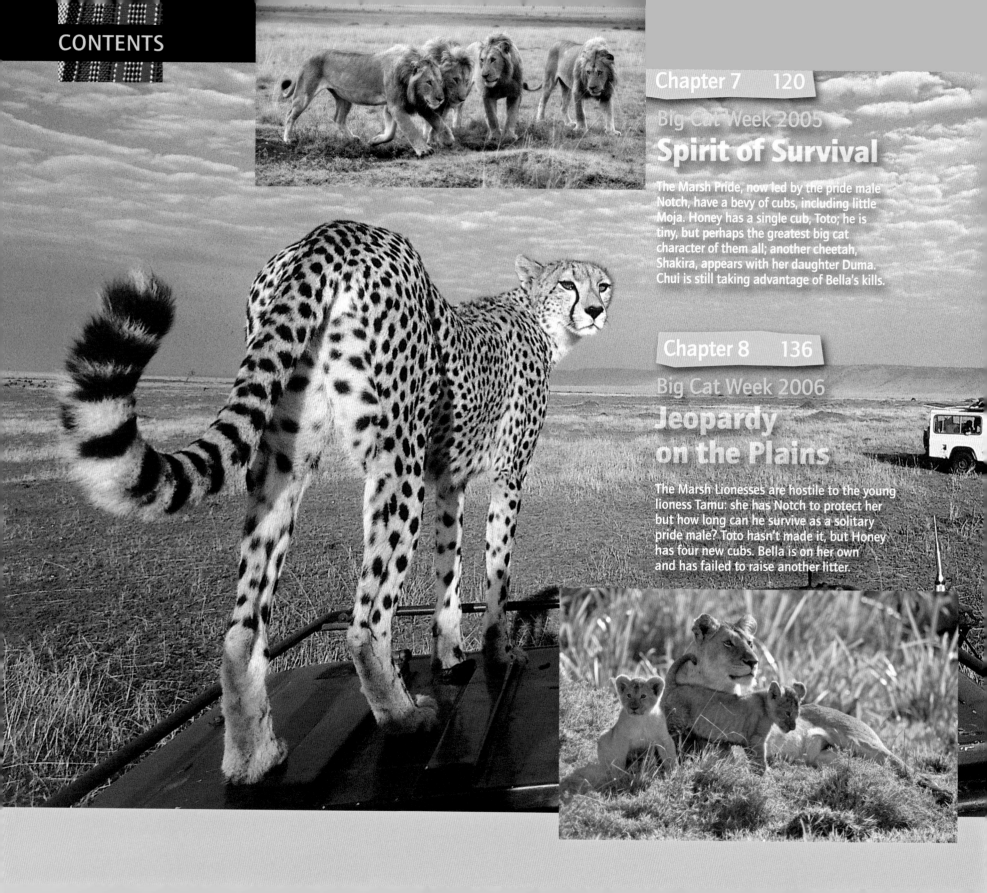

# CONTENTS

# Stars of

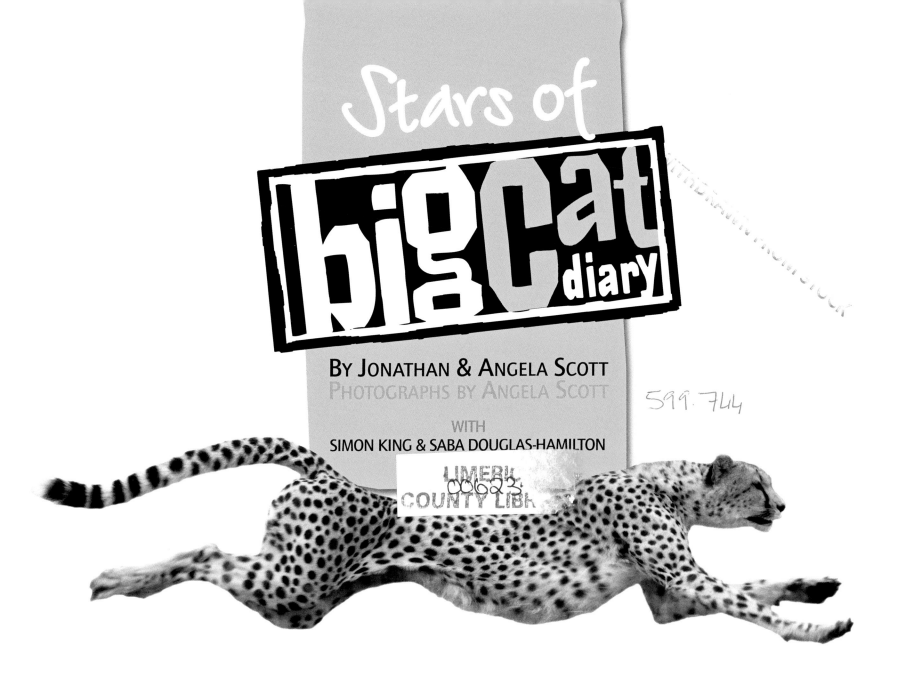

# Stars of bigcat diary

BY JONATHAN & ANGELA SCOTT

PHOTOGRAPHS BY ANGELA SCOTT

WITH

SIMON KING & SABA DOUGLAS-HAMILTON

EVANS
MITCHELL
BOOKS

# CONTENTS

To our children Alia and David, and daughter-in-law Tara, who have grown up with this story and helped to make the Mara such a special place for our family.

**Publishers**
Evans Mitchell Books
The Old Forge
16 Church Street
Rickmansworth, Herts
WD3 1DH United Kingdom
info@embooks.co.uk
www.embooks.co.uk

© Evans Mitchell Books 2009

**Text & Photographs**
© ScottFree Enterprises 2009

**Editor** Caroline Taggart

**Design** Darren Westlake at **TU ink** www.tuink.co.uk

**Origination, Printing and Binding**
Passavia, Germany

**ISBN** 978-1-901268-42-3

## Big Cat Live 2008
## End of an Era

The Marsh Pride have three new males, with White Eye and Red (Mama Lugga) now the matriarchs. Honey has died between series, but her 'boys' survive; Shakira has an enormous litter of six cubs. We meet 'the Jackson Five' – Bella's extended family.

The story continues. Notch has joined up with younger male relatives to form a powerful alliance and take over another pride; both Honey and Bella have left successful offspring who will ensure that the Big Cat story continues.

# Big Cat Country

Mara River Camp

Mara River

Mara River

Kichwa Tembo Camp

Leopard Gorge

Fig Tree Ridge

Little Governor's Camp

Musiara Gate

Governor's Camp

Olare Orok

SIRIA ESCARPMENT

Bila Shaka Lugga

Rhino Ridge

PARADISE PLAIN

Mara Intrepids Camp

MARA TRIANGLE

Serena Lodge

Talek River

KENYA

TANZANIA

SERENGETI NATIONAL PARK

Mara River

Mara New Bridge

Sand River

AFRICA

Kenya

Lake Victoria

Masai Mara National Reserve

Tanzania

## KEY

Musiara Marsh

▲ Camp

// Regular wildebeest crossing places

⟋ Reserve Boundary

▭ Gate

▬ Airstrip

North

It is September 1996 when the opening titles of **Big Cat Diary** roll for the first time, revealing Africa's big cats in all their **magnificence**.

You can feel your pulse racing
as the music soars; there is a hint
of the deep, throaty cry of Masai
warriors who still at times test their
courage against the king of beasts
in this part of Kenya.

Two huge male lions go head
to head, battling tooth and claw,
the dust flying as they manoeuvre
for position; a cheetah explodes
towards camera, its feet beating
a blistering tattoo on the dry earth,
while a solitary leopard climbs
higher into a tree, smooth as silk:
just a glimpse, nothing more, but
with a creature as beautiful and
mysterious as this it is enough...

To be able to write this book, I needed to hear the voices of the other presenters and to remind myself of exactly what our audience had been seeing over the course of the years.

To do that, I sat down and watched all the tapes. Suddenly I was the audience, sitting in my living room in Nairobi, the curtains drawn, shutting out the Africa that has become my home, a wilderness garden rolling away towards the distinctive blue arc of the Ngong Hills – Karen Blixen country. As I watched each programme, I felt the magic building – the music upbeat, providing energy and pace to the images, connecting me to the pulsing rhythm that is such a part of Africa and the thing I love.

Simon's custom-built filming door and roof mount allow him a 360-degree view; his sheer joy in filming wildlife is infectious.

The series opens on the west side of the Mara River in an area of the Masai Mara Game Reserve known as the Triangle. This is cheetah country, a vast open plain with scattered trees resembling Africa's quintessential flat-topped acacias, though they are in fact balanites – desert dates. To the west, rising high above the sun-kissed plains looms the blue knife edge of the Siria Escarpment where Angie and I were married, and beyond lies the great Serengeti National Park, ancestral home of the wildebeest and zebra migration. I know of no more beautiful place in the world...

A massive thunderhead dwarfs presenter Simon King's vehicle as he races across the plains to introduce the first programme in what will become one of the longest running

and most successful wildlife series ever seen on television. Simon and I had first met in the 1980s when he was planning a film on Kali the lioness, a member of a pride that I had been following for many years. Although only in his twenties, Simon was already one of the most accomplished cameramen/producers of his generation. He had been born in Kenya and loved the Mara and its big cats as much as I did. But we both knew that wildlife film-making was changing: reality television were the new buzz words. It was time to try something different.

Cut to Simon in his vehicle: 'This is the Masai Mara in Kenya, one of the best places on earth for watching wildlife. But in this series we are going to be looking at it in an entirely new way. Over the next six weeks we are going to be following in intimate detail the lives of Africa's big cats, sending back a weekly report – a diary of their hardships and good fortunes as they happen.'

*Big Cat Diary* was the brainchild of Keith Scholey, who had a highly successful career as a producer, then went on to head the BBC Natural History Unit. Keith knew the Mara intimately and had produced films of his own here on leopards and wild dogs. He knew the Marsh Pride, too, and saw the potential that the Mara had to offer for a wildlife soap opera featuring the big cats, taking his lead from hugely popular programmes such as *Animal Hospital*, which enthralled their audience with intimate and emotional stories about the lives of individual animals.

Imagine the excitement we all felt as the *Big Cat* team assembled in the Mara for that first series. None of us was quite sure what to expect – all we knew was that this was to be a wildlife series with a difference. Using presenters would add a more intimate feel, making the programmes more personal, as if you were there on safari with us.

Two males standing tall on Paradise Plain. At about four years old they are ready to challenge for a pride of their own.

Key to the success of the series would be to focus on just a few cats. With the help of drivers and guides from the safari camps and lodges, we had identified which of the big cats we hoped to feature before the first camera rolled. The Marsh Lions were an obvious choice. They occupied a territory of around 50 sq km (20 sq miles) bordering the Mara River on the west (where the *Big Cat* Camp was positioned) and spreading north to the perennial spring feeding Musiara Marsh, which gave the pride its name. To the east lay the core of the Marsh Pride territory, a sparsely wooded drainage line or lugga called Bila Shaka, a Swahili expression meaning 'without fail'. This is where the pride could often be found, and where the lionesses most often chose to give birth to their cubs.

In 1996 the Marsh Pride was in a state of flux: the old pride males had disappeared and as yet new males had failed to establish a sense of order, so we needed to identify a second pride we could work with in case our first choice failed to deliver the action we were hoping for. The Big Pride was aptly named, with seven adult females, four pride males and 16 cubs – 27 lions in total. I would share the task of reporting on the lions' story with Simon, who would also follow two families of cheetahs, a female called Fundi, who had two cubs of around a year old, and a younger female called Kidogo, whose two cubs were not quite four months.

This left me with the leopard, a creature full of contradictions that make it hard to define and even harder to film.

Leopards are solitary, though they do at times socialise; they are hunters both of the dark and of the daylight hours; they will invest time in stalking a hare or a hyrax, then kill something as large as an adult topi if the opportunity arises; consummate predators, they are also so shy and retiring that they can vanish from view before you even see them. This was the cat that threatened to make or break *Big Cat Diary*. Without the leopard we would fail before we had even begun. In fact we might never have considered making the series if it hadn't been for Half-Tail.

Angie and I had followed Half-Tail ever since she first appeared as a newly independent two-year-old at the end of the 1980s. Nobody was sure where she had come from, but now her territory lay to the north of the Marsh Pride's, an area I knew intimately from the years when I lived at Mara River Camp. In those days Leopard Gorge and Fig Tree Ridge – two areas so naturally picturesque and scenic that they almost feel like a film set – were a part of nearly every game drive; now, as the heart of Half-Tail's territory, they were going to make a wonderful filming location.

When we began filming *Big Cat Diary*, Half-Tail was about eight years old and had a female cub called Zawadi. Zawadi, or Shadow as she became known to viewers, was seven months old: beautiful, inquisitive, mischievous and playful. Zawadi is a Swahili word meaning gift – and what a gift this young leopard would prove to be. The decision to call her Shadow was a result of our producers' believing that the audience wouldn't be able to relate to her Swahili name – yet it is music on the ears and I was disappointed to have to bow to a convention that would later change; I never got used to calling Zawadi by her English name.

A production as large and as complex as *Big Cat Diary* became possible only by calling on the expertise of many different individuals, not least of whom were our game spotters, whose job it was to go out at the crack of dawn each morning and locate the cats. There were six camera crews, some dedicated to individual cats and others to filming sync pieces with Simon and me. Two editors and their assistants logged and compiled sequences back at camp as soon as they had been shot, with three producers assigned to create and

Half-Tail: the Mara's most famous leopard

Amber: also known as Queen because of her regal bearing

Chui: Bella's mischievous and irrepressible son

Scar: everybody's idea of a magnificent-looking lion

follow the story line for each cat. At the end of each week someone flew back to NHU headquarters in Bristol, clutching the precious tapes to be aired a few days later.

Each of our big cats would pose its own challenges to filming. Lions are never happier than when spending much of the day doing absolutely nothing. Then just as the light begins to fade the lions yawn and stretch, a signal that they are about to become active and are preparing to hunt. It was incredibly frustrating to have to pack up and head back to camp just as things were getting interesting. It didn't mean viewers missed out on the action, however – we just called in the night shift.

In the first episode, Simon explains how this works: 'We can't use ordinary lights on the cats at night because they'd dazzle both the predators and their prey. But the night team is using infra-red technology, lights that are invisible to the human eye and the eyes of other animals, but perfectly clear to our specially sensitive cameras.' After he has said this piece to camera, I am seen driving out into the darkness to demonstrate how it is done. With my headlights covered with infra-red filters and a small infra-red camera on the roof of my vehicle feeding an image on to a monitor above my steering wheel, I can see where I am going – sort of. To see off to the side I have to don a pair of heavy and cumbersome night-vision goggles normally employed by the military for night manoeuvres.

How driver-guide Andrew Karanja navigated the night crew around in the darkness each evening I just don't know. He somehow managed to track the lions as they disappeared into the blackness without getting hopelessly lost. It was quite a feat; each morning we would pass him and the crew on their way home and salute them after a quick chat about what had been happening and where they had left the cats. During the course of the series the night crew caught all three of our big cats on tape, providing some fascinating insights into the nocturnal habits of our stars.

Despite the wonderful images, the excitement and dramas, during that first series none of us could have believed how successful *Big Cat Diary* would become. Twelve years on this is a journey that all who have worked on the series are proud to have been part of. Although some of our star cats have passed on – Half-Tail and Amber, Kali and Scar, Kike and Toto, then Honey, to name just a few – this is their story and a tribute to the making of a remarkable television programme.

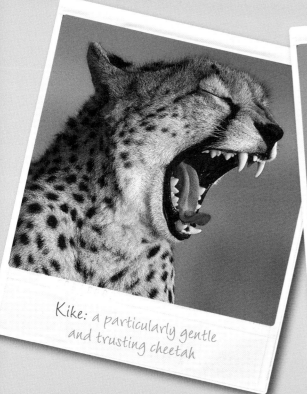

Kike: a particularly gentle and trusting cheetah

Toto: a youngster who captured the hearts of the nation

Honey: one of the most successful mothers in the Mara

# The Big Cat
# Kingdom

Fireworks from the Marsh Pride gave some bite and edge to the first programme in Series 1. Simon had located four adult lionesses accompanied by three subadults, around two years of age – a female and two males – as well as two year-old cubs. But there was no sign of any pride males. The previous territory holders – two ageing males – had been chased away, but as yet a new coalition had failed to assert their right to the Marsh Pride territory. Then one morning Simon and his spotters found two magnificent male lions moving with a sense of purpose along the edge of the riverine forest bordering the marsh. They acted so confidently that Simon felt sure that this was the missing piece of the jigsaw defining the Marsh Pride. One of the males had a magnificent ginger mane, the other a broad band of black running like a saddle across his shoulders and around his chest. Simon filmed the two scent-marking bushes and raking the base of a tree, laying down a marker to any other males in the area that this was their domain.

The lionesses were lying in the grass about 200 m (220 yds) away, and when they spotted the ginger-maned male 'standing tall' at the edge of the forest they immediately advanced towards him, running with that low, rolling gait that says 'watch out'. The male turned broadside, flaunting the sheer size of his body and holding himself stiffly upright, his mane draped like a rug around his neck. But as all four females closed on him, with the two young males bringing up the rear, he ran. The leading lioness reached out and swiped at Ginger Mane's back legs, raking his bottom with her outstretched claws, slowing him down and forcing him to turn and defend himself. The females rushed him as one, biting and clawing, prompting him to turn again and run for his life.

Generally lions use threat and intimidation rather than actual fighting to settle their differences, baring their formidable canines and grunting and growling to scare off a rival.

**The maternal instinct**
Lionesses will often gang up on a male intruder. Male lions are much larger than females, so the mothers are sometimes risking their lives in order to protect their cubs.

**Above right:** Two of the Marsh Lionesses alert to prey. By hunting communally, lions can pull down large, dangerous prey such buffalo and zebra and defend their kills against the numerous spotted hyenas.
**Opposite:** A lioness carries a four-week-old-cub to a new hiding place. All the big cats use this method of transport when their cubs are small and helpless.

Satisfied with their collective show of force, the lionesses headed back to their cubs. But by now the black-maned male had arrived, ready and willing to join in the fray. Ginger Mane charged back with a frightening turn of speed for such a large animal, roaring in defiance, determined to let the lionesses know that he and his companion were laying claim to the Marsh Pride's territory.

That evening Simon spoke to one of the drivers from Kichwa Tembo Camp, on the other side of the river in the Mara Triangle. Apparently earlier in the year the Kichwa Tembo Pride males had disappeared; nobody knew where they had gone. Then a few days ago they had reappeared. Maybe the mystery males were from the Kichwa Tembo Pride. The following morning we set off to find out, and sure enough when we arrived on the other side of the river we found Ginger Mane and Black Mane lying confidently in their old territory. It is not uncommon for males to try to expand their realm of influence and for as long as I have lived in the Mara males from the Marsh Pride and the Kichwa Tembo Pride have contested ownership of these two territories. Though the river forms a natural boundary, lions can easily navigate a way across the maze of stepping stones revealed in the dry season. If they need to they simply swim, albeit

wary of the giant crocodiles that inhabit the river.

On this occasion the males had had to swim, as one of the things that is firmly etched in my mind about this first series is the weather. It poured. It was as if we had been ambushed by the long rains that normally begin towards the end of March. But this was September and, even though the Mara expects to receive scattered showers around this time, this was much more than the usual so-called 'grass rains'. In one programme we see Simon standing out of the roof hatch of his camera vehicle clad in a poncho as the water pours off his safari wagon. Drenched by the storm, he explains that the Mara is experiencing more rainfall at this time of year than in the last 30 years.

The ground by now had the consistency of chewing gum, making it almost impossible to drive without getting stuck; at times it was fruitless to try to film without damaging the equipment. Before long the entrance to our camp had been churned to a quagmire. At one point hurricane-force winds swept through. Tent frames were bent like matchsticks and our sound man returned in the evening to find that his tent had been tossed 70 m (75 yds) through the air and deposited in the river – tables, bed, the lot! Some of his possessions were fished out of the water; most were a write-off.

# big cat diary

## Bringing the series to life

### Going digital
Digital cameras give greater latitude when filming in low light – a huge bonus with big cats, who are often active around dawn and dusk. The Canon HJ40 stabilised lenses are superb for action shots.

### Keep it clean
Dust can be a nightmare when filming in Africa. Above (l. to r.) Mark Yates, Chris Watson, Warwick Sloss and Dave Parkinson check their cameras and sound gear.

One of the things that we set out to do from the beginning was to make our programmes different. With the best wildlife cameramen in the world – Simon, Martyn Colbeck, Richard Matthews and Gavin Thurston all filmed for us on that first series – and a location packed with animals, it would have been easy to settle for the *Wildlife on One* approach – beautifully shot half-hour documentaries with a strong storyline eloquently narrated by Sir David Attenborough. Using presenters and providing glimpses of camp life and how it felt to work on *Big Cat Diary* helped to move things along, and our editors Andy Chastney and Steve White played a crucial role in creating pace and energy – they worked miracles in cutting sequences together within days. Some people felt uncomfortable with the 'stings' – the fast-cut imagery that acted as time transitions between segments – but they added a more modern approach to our journey.

At one point a beautiful aerial shot of the *Big Cat* Camp captures the thrill

we all felt, living out in the wilds of Africa for weeks on end. Simon picks up the commentary as the aeroplane carrying our cameraman swoops low overhead: 'For the six weeks of our transmission 40 people are living under canvas or African skies. All the trappings of television production have been transported to the Masai Mara to make sure the programmes are ready for transmission within the week.' We had hoped that showing the programmes virtually live would create even more excitement for our audience. In the end we found that this was an unnecessary and costly complication which would not be repeated if a second series was commissioned. But for the moment we were in a prime-time slot on BBC1 usually reserved for 'light entertainment' – wildlife programmes were traditionally thought of as attracting the more conservative, special-interest audience usually associated with BBC2.

Simon's greatest challenge was to keep in contact with the two cheetah families. Fundi and the older cubs were favouring the dense acacia country where they could find plenty of impalas to prey on. But in addition to the problem of the energy-sapping heat which swiftly traded places with the rains, the terrain was a minefield of rocks and seething with tsetse flies which have a bite like the sting of a hornet. It had been days since the cheetah crew had last found Fundi and in Simon's commentary his concern is beginning to tell: 'The longer it goes on the less chance I think we have of ever finding them again. But we can only keep looking.'

It is hard to convey just how tedious and frustrating times such as these can be; naturally enough the audience wants to see great action and engaging stories rather than listen to us telling them how difficult it is to find and follow our stars. Fortunately one of the strengths of *Big Cat Diary* is having the option to switch between the three cats: if the cheetahs go quiet we can always focus on the leopards, and if they are lying asleep in a tree then it's time to see what the lions are doing.

The Big Pride was proving a joy to work with; so many lions and their cubs travelling together made irresistible viewing. It was one of those times in a pride's history when everything falls into place. I did one piece to camera with virtually the whole pride crowded round my car, nearly 20 lions perched on a termite mound. You could feel their energy; they exuded such confidence that they appeared invincible. With four pride males to defend the territory and a tightly bonded crèche to nurture their 16 cubs, the six lionesses (a seventh was heavily pregnant) were nearing their domain's capacity to provide sufficient food for their family. This was evident from the fact that one young female had been forced to live as an outcast as she struggled to find acceptance within the pride. This younger lioness tried desperately to maintain contact with her natal pride, but was generally received with open hostility by her relatives.

The Big Pride with part of a large crèche of cubs. Lionesses with cubs of a similar age nurture their young communally, increasing their chances of survival.

By the age of eight weeks
a cub is introduced into the
social world of its pride.

Having managed to trace the origins of the two big male lions who had invaded the Marsh Pride territory, we realised that there was little point in continuing to follow their story – unless they decided to come back to 'our' side of the river. It involved too much travel time and Simon was already struggling to keep in touch with Fundi. Kidogo and her cubs, however, were proving a delight. Cubs of this age – four to five months – are just so full of life: irrepressible and boisterous. At one point one of them jumped on to the bonnet of Simon's car, an adventurous leap for such a young cat: 'From my point of view it is a magnificent privilege to be treated with such indifference by a totally wild animal.' This incident would prove to be the forerunner of many encounters with car-climbing cheetahs for both Simon and me.

A far less pleasurable experience soon tested Simon's resolve never to interfere with what happens to our big cats. One morning Kidogo's two cubs were scrambling about in an acacia bush, having a riotous game of 'I'm the king of the castle', when the little female slipped head first in the crotch of the bush, trapping her front left foot. We see her hanging there, her leg grotesquely twisted, squealing in pain. Her brother mistakenly thinks this is all part of the game, an invitation to play, and he grabs and tugs at her while their mother watches, unsure of what to do. 'I was in a complete panic,' says Simon. 'There was nothing I could do with Kidogo nearby – it would cause her dreadful upset – but my instinct was to dash over to try to help the youngster. I felt sure her leg would have been permanently damaged by the force of the fall.'

After what seems like an eternity the little cub manages to struggle far enough back up the tree to free herself, and no sooner is she down than she is charging around with her brother again. 'Any time any of the cubs goes near a tree I have palpitations,' Simon comments. We were beginning to express our emotions.

There was some good news at the beginning of Programme 4, when we were able to reveal that a new litter of cubs had been born to one of the Marsh Lionesses. When we first saw them the cubs were about three weeks old and their eyes had just opened: little bundles of spotted fur with pug faces and small, rounded ears – simply adorable. While we were all excited by this unexpected discovery we were naturally anxious about their chances of survival. The cubs' fathers had disappeared, leaving a dangerous vacuum that in itself might pose problems. As it was, the lionesses faced the prospect of a protracted war with the Kichwa Tembo males, who would certainly kill these cubs if they found them.

To add to the lionesses' woes their area was looking increasingly barren. In the wake of all the rain the great herds of wildebeest and zebra that form what we know as 'the migration' had moved on, forcing the pride to subsist on wart hogs or to target larger prey that generally proved too difficult for a small pride such as this. We watched them chase a giraffe with a newborn calf without success and then Martyn Colbeck managed to film one of them making a desperate lunge at an eland – largest of all antelopes – they had cornered in a croton thicket. The bull – they average 500–600 kg (1,100–1,300 lb) but can weigh up to a tonne (2,200 lb) – galloped off, brushing aside the lioness like a powerful rugby player bursting through a despairing tackle.

Above: The Big Pride feeding on a wildebeest kill. The presence of the migration provides the lions with plenty of easy prey.
Below: A group of young males move towards cover to rest during the heat of the day.

# big cat diary

# Camera – and action!

In hindsight what is very evident in these early programmes is how formally Simon and I presented our pieces to camera. These were taped by a sync crew who specialised in working with presenters and each piece was carefully scripted and set up in advance. The idea was that our sync pieces would help to link important sequences while still giving the sense of us being in the field with the cats that we were commenting on. At times the process was agonisingly slow and painstaking – witness the fact that on one occasion Zawadi leapt onto a fallen tree right next to my car in a perfect position for a two-shot, but we were unable to capture the moment – it hadn't been discussed and scripted. That, though, was all part of the learning process.

As I sit and watch some of these programmes 12 years later it is interesting to see the way our producers and cameramen were trying to make the relationship between us and the audience more intimate. There are over-the-shoulder shots of Martyn Colbeck filming lions, which really work – highlighting how 'removed' and impersonal things appeared at times with either Simon or me leaning out of our cars and talking to a camera vehicle positioned on the other side of our cats. Sure, you can tell that we are there watching proceedings, but it isn't as personal as we would have liked. Snippets of radio chat from Peter Blackwell, who was driving Martyn's camera vehicle, and from David Breed as he ensured that Simon was in the best position to tape the action when it kicked off certainly help to give a sense of immediacy and an insight into what it is taking to create the shows. But these intimate moments are few and far between at this point.

Rather than the actuality style we were ultimately aiming for there were long pieces of narration, albeit packed with interesting information on cat behaviour. We recorded these each week in a vehicle tucked away in a patch of forest close to camp. The biggest challenge was in getting clean sound amidst the constant coming and going of safari vehicles and aeroplanes.

For the past two weeks Half-Tail and Zawadi had camped out along Fig Tree Ridge, enabling us to find them every single day. This area is a magnet to lions and hyenas, which sometimes commandeer the caves and rocky crevices as a hiding place for their cubs; on one occasion our leopards had to slip away when two lionesses from the Gorge Pride wandered along the ridge, scent-marking and roaring out a warning to Half-Tail and her daughter to move on.

Zawadi was always full of mischief and I had to chuckle when she hauled herself 4 m (13 ft) up a boscia tree to feast on an impala that Half-Tail had killed, only to lose her grip and plummet like a stone for a soft landing in the long grass. Later than evening the night crew arrived to film our leopard stars. The hyenas had forced Zawadi to seek refuge in the top of an acacia bush, while Half-Tail continued to snooze in the boscia, her kill safely wedged beside her as one of the hyenas nosed around for scraps dropped from the leopards' larder. Once the last hyena had headed off into the night Half-Tail descended and called Zawadi to her, prompting scenes of delightful exuberance.

At dawn the following morning we arrived to find mother and daughter engaged in the same playful manner, providing us with a window into a rarely witnessed social side of the leopard's behaviour. Their play was rough at times now that Zawadi was older: pounces and grabs followed by bites to the neck, each lunging at the other's throat to press home an advantage. Sometimes Half-Tail would clasp Zawadi tight, pinning her down on the ground or using her claws to restrain her. Over and over again, pounce, grab, bite – so quick – but that is the way leopards overpower their prey. And when they fight over territory it is a real cat fight, no holds barred, a white-knuckle affair that can leave an opponent seriously injured – even dead. Zawadi was learning something of the harsh existence that a lone predator must face, where securing a meal and protecting a territory are vital to survival. Her hunting skills developed quickly. By the end of the series we found her with a hyrax she had

**Denizens of the shadows**
Half-Tail's beautiful coat of spots and rosettes breaks up her outline and makes her almost invisible in the long grass. A leopard could be crouched only a few metres away and you would not see it – unless it moved.

killed at the entrance to Leopard Gorge.

To add to the cheetah crew's difficulties, Fundi was still favouring the dense acacia thickets, acting more like a leopard as she hunted young and pregnant impalas. Simon highlights the dangers of this tactic: 'When walking through thick cover a cheetah is more at risk from leopards, lions and other predators that use the bush and woods for shade during the day.' Leopards are one of the biggest dangers to adult cheetahs in woodland areas and will kill and eat their spotted relative whenever the opportunity arises. By contrast Simon thought of Kidogo as more of a 'text book' cheetah: she tended to keep to a relatively small home range, avoided dense cover where her young cubs might be exposed to danger, and hunted on the open plains, targeting almost exclusively Thomson's gazelles.

Watching the same cat day after day you live and breathe their every move and begin to identify the individual threads that pattern their lives: there is plenty of time for reflection. In general the favourite prey of a hungry cheetah is a single, unobservant, rather weary Thomson's gazelle. Adult male gazelles spend much of their time marking and defending their territories, making them prime targets. Added to this, the rains had unleashed a tide of births among the Tommies, so there were plenty of young fawns

wobbling on unsteady feet within minutes of being born, then crouching chin to the ground in a posture of concealment, allowing their mother to continue feeding until she was ready to suckle her youngster. To an experienced cheetah these newborns are easy prey to be run down without even hitting top gear and are sometimes released to young cubs to allow them to practise their hunting skills. Simon and Richard Matthews captured some stunning action sequences of Kidogo, following every twist and turn as she used her long spotted tail as a rudder to maintain her balance when pursuing her prey.

At four months Kidogo's cubs were paying close attention every time their mother hunted, rushing in the moment she managed to trip and anchor a gazelle. On one occasion a Tommy tripped and fell, injuring its leg. The male cub immediately grabbed the stricken gazelle by the throat and pinned it to the ground while his sister looked on nervously. Meanwhile a Masai youth strode across the plains barely 50 m (55 yds) away, radio playing, indifferent to the cats. Kidogo watched but did not flee – witness to the herdsmen's tolerance of predators that do not threaten their livelihood.

The Marsh Lions continued to struggle to find sufficient food for their cubs. At times they targeted the numerous waterbuck that frequent the marsh while remaining constantly on the look-out for wart hogs – their staple diet in the absence of the wildebeest and zebra herds. On one occasion Simon found the lionesses on the hunt, but this time their target wasn't a wart hog: it was another lioness, a youngster who had lain hidden in the grass and was now under attack from four full-grown lionesses who not only outnumbered her but were bigger and stronger too – a lioness doesn't reach full size until around four or five years of age. It was no contest, with the younger lioness desperately trying to defend herself. As she faced one attacker the others pressed in around her, lashing out with their claws, raking and biting at her thighs and hindquarters. Perhaps she was a younger relative whom the lionesses might grudgingly tolerate as long as she kept her distance. Like the mothers in the Big Pride the Marsh Lionesses had young cubs to look after; there was no room for an additional mouth to feed.

The young lioness eventually managed to break free and limped off down the main road, a lonely figure with nowhere to call home, bearing new wounds to add to the partially healed ones from previous violent encounters. The roars of the Marsh Lionesses rang in her ears. Ahead lay uncertainty: wherever she roamed she faced hostility, from either the Masai or the Big Pride. It was a stark reminder of how tough and unforgiving the life of a single lion can be. Not in terms of finding food – a lioness is quite capable of hunting on her own so long as she stays fit and healthy. But without the collective power of pride members to help ward off the ever-present danger posed by strange males (and females from other prides), and lacking the opportunity to form a crèche with female relatives with cubs of a similar age, it is almost impossible for a single lioness to raise her young to independence.

Throughout the series the night crew continued to deliver remarkable footage, adding a totally different element to our programmes and revealing a world that is rarely witnessed. There are dramatic scenes of hyenas forcing the Marsh Pride from a topi kill; the Big Pride gambolling about with their cubs or successfully hunting gazelles; as well as some lovely intimate shots of Half-Tail and Zawadi at play and Kidogo and her cubs giving the Big Pride the slip after dark. It is illuminating to see the advantage that the cats' superb night vision gives them; the lions are often able to stalk within metres of their prey in the open, particularly on a moonless night.

At one point we see the lionesses ambush a herd of Grant's gazelles, one of the swiftest and long-winded of all the animals. Slow to rise from the ground and confused in the darkness, one of the gazelles is quickly tripped and pulled down again, leading to a scrap between adults and youngsters over the spoils. The sounds are blood-curdling as the lions fight furiously for their share of the kill, which is devoured within 10 minutes.

One night, after the Big Pride have killed a

zebra, the lionesses line up on one side of the carcass while one of the males holds pride of place opposite them. The carcass is stripped of its meat, prompting the male to drive the lionesses away, although he still allows the cubs – his cubs – to feed with him. This makes sense. The lionesses are not related to the male. They can hunt again. Permitting the cubs to share in his meal protects the male's investment in the lives of his descendants.

The lions had killed close to a Masai enkang – a thornbush corral or boma enclosing a number of dung-covered houses and livestock. A dog barks in alarm as torches flash in the darkness: the noise of the lion's squabbling has roused the herdsmen from their sleep. A group of men clad only in red shukas and armed with spears emerge at the edge of the enclosure. One of them slams the long metal shaft of his spear into the ground – the intention is clear; there is business to attend to. At that the lions begin to move away and the Masai drift back into their boma. Within minutes,

**Above:** As the Marsh Pride feed on a kill, vultures gather in the tree tops, waiting for their chance to pick the carcass clean.
**Right:** A male lion can eat almost a quarter of his body weight at any one time.

though, the night erupts with sound again as hyenas close in on the kill, whooping and giggling at the prospect of an easy meal. But not for long. If there is one thing that drives a male lion to distraction it is the sight of hyenas, particularly when food is at stake. The pride male charges back into the fray, scattering the hyenas in all directions, picking up the remains of the kill and carrying it off into the darkness.

The young lioness who has been exiled from the pride now approaches cautiously. The male looks up but does not challenge her – she is no threat to him and in time he will mate with her and perhaps sire her first litter of cubs. In the meantime, at least she is able to get a little nourishment from the scraps he has left.

By the last week of filming, the Marsh Pride's three tiny cubs were thriving. At around six weeks old they were able to walk and play and were a delight to watch. We knew of another three litters, all born within four weeks of each other in the same area along Bila Shaka. No wonder the lionesses had reacted so belligerently to the appearance of the Kichwa Tembo males – they had all been pregnant. But we also knew that it would be a miracle if any of these tiny cubs survived. When new males invaded the territory – and they inevitably would – they would hunt these youngsters down and kill them, bringing the mothers back into oestrus and allowing the males to breed as soon as possible.

For me one of the most memorable and exciting moments of this first series was when one of our spotters located Beauty, Half-Tail's oldest surviving cub and Zawadi's elder sister. I was ecstatic. Beauty had been a wonderful cub to work with and Angie and I had followed her for weeks at a time when she was young. But as she grew older it was all too apparent that she lacked the confidence around vehicles that her mother and younger sister possessed. Once she became fully independent she did everything she could to avoid vehicles, reacting aggressively whenever a car came racing towards her. Before long nobody could find her – she had retreated into that secret world that so many leopards inhabit, a world where man and his vehicles are the enemy and viewed as a threat.

Our spotter could tell by the sounds coming from a clump of croton bushes not far from Leopard Gorge that leopards were mating. The following day the courting couple moved to a more accessible place, though it was still a minefield of long grass and rocks. Simon was the closest cameraman to the gorge at that time, so he abandoned his cheetah quest and rushed over to cover the mating pair for us. The male was so large that he made Beauty look like a cub. He was young – perhaps four or five years old – and showing just the beginnings of a loose fold of skin along his throat, the dewlap that characterises older males. Beauty continually initiated matings, sinuously winding herself around the male and pushing up under his chin as a cub does when begging its mother for attention or food. The pair mated four or five times as the night closed in around us. The noises emanating from the male were extraordinary – he let out a stuttering, gurgling, growl-type rumble from his throat as he bit down over Beauty's neck and climaxed. This was the sound that our spotter had heard and knew instantly that it was something special, as it is rare to see leopards mating.

**Left:** Beauty, Half-Tail's daughter, in long red oat grass near Leopard Gorge.
**Above:** At five or six months old, Beauty loved to play around vehicles.

Left:
Balanites trees –
which are common in the
Mara Triangle – can offer cheetah
cubs a refuge from predators.
Main picture: Lions often rest up in rocky
outcrops during the heat of the day.
Opposite: Lions do sometimes
climb trees, although they lack
the leopard's grace.

## As the series draws to a close Simon sums it all up:

'We've spent 11,000 man hours in the field. In that time we've shot over 80 km of video tape, utilised three tonnes of equipment and driven over 40,000 km. We've had 360 punctures and got stuck 420 times. We worked our way through 8,000 litres of water and 1,000 loaves of bread, and finished each programme in time — just.' He also confides to the audience his feelings about watching Kidogo and her fast-growing cubs: 'It has been the blossoming of these cats which has given me the greatest pleasure over our weeks here. Their tireless spirit and sense of fun in this harsh environment have been inspirational.'

It was with real sadness that Simon headed back to camp. Angie and I are fortunate to live in Kenya and think of the Mara as our second home. While we waited to hear if there would be another series of *Big Cat Diary* we could continue to follow the lives of our favourite wild creatures.

wherever I stop in this vast plain
— they'll find us!

# Sunlight and Shadows

'They are among the most powerful, the fastest, most dynamic and compelling creatures on earth – the big cats are back,' proclaims Simon at the start of Series 2. *Big Cat Diary* had competed against the best of the UK soap operas, not to mention Manchester United playing in the European Cup, and still emerged with its head held high. But this time we were not on BBC1 – the commissioners were playing safe, not yet convinced that *Big Cat Diary* was ready for the 'big time'. Instead we were given a comfortable Sunday afternoon slot on BBC2, home of dedicated natural-history viewers across the UK. The series had proved a success on the other side of the ocean too and our co-producers the Discovery Channel had recommissioned it for their dedicated wildlife channel, Animal Planet. We were all delighted to be reunited as a team – there had been such a buzz working on the first series that we could hardly wait for another chance to prove just what a remarkable place the Masai Mara is for watching big cats – and that *Big Cat Diary* had the potential to be an even bigger success.

# big cat diary

## Cheetah

## fact file...

The tail acts as a rudder, helping with manoeuvrability and balance.

**Face to face**
The tear marks running down a cheetah's face seem to be an important visual element when confronting or appeasing a rival or mate.

**On the alert**
Termite mounds make natural look-out points, allowing a cheetah to advertise its presence, and to spot prey – and danger.

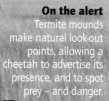

# Amber
## did you know?

At the beginning of Programme 1 Simon introduces the audience to Amber, an adult female cheetah: 'She is mother to three well-grown cubs and an experienced and accomplished hunter, which is just as well because at the moment she has her work cut out for her.'

What Simon doesn't tell the audience is that this particular female is something of a legend in the Mara, known to the drivers and guides as Queen in tribute to her habit of jumping onto the bonnet of vehicles and sitting there in regal pose as she surveys her surroundings. It simply isn't possible during filming to delve into the history of this remarkable feline,

whom I had watched as a young cub in the Rhino Ridge area during the dry season of 1987. At that time she was one of five cubs. Some months later the family moved north and the mother was seen hunting around Leopard Gorge. Not long afterwards, she was mortally wounded, probably by a leopard or lion; leopards are a major cause of death of adult cheetahs in the wooded areas. The cubs were seven to eight months old at the time of their mother's death, far too young to survive on their own, so the reserve authorities took the decision to provide the cubs with 'kills' – gazelles and impalas shot by rangers – until the young cheetahs were capable of surviving on their own, and ensuring that they did not end up in captivity. So Amber grew up believing that vehicles meant the possibility of a meal. That is how she became so relaxed around us – and earned her name as Queen.

Unlike the first series, when the Marsh Pride had lacked the reassuring presence of pride males, this year they promised to deliver. The four lionesses that viewers had already met had been joined by a younger relative, making five in all – Bump Nose, the Old One, Kali, Notch and Blondie – and much to our delight they had a gaggle of eight ten-week-old-cubs in tow. The cubs had been sired by two new pride males known as Brown Mane (later renamed Scar) and Scruffy. The males could not have looked more different. Scar was a magnificent animal, large-bodied and resplendent in a luxuriant ginger mane that was turning black on his chest. Scruffy was so called because of a mane that would remain sparse all his life rather than thickening and darkening with age.

But looks can be deceiving. Scruffy was a warrior, braver and more combative than his regal companion, even though he was younger. Perhaps the two males had joined forces as nomads or been born to different lionesses within the same pride: the majority of male coalitions in the Mara consist of just two lions and in many instances they are not related. On his own a male struggles to take over and hold a pride. Together Scar and Scruffy had a future.

While Simon was responsible for the cheetahs and we continued to share the lions' story, I was reunited with Zawadi, now a magnificent two-and-a-half-year-old leopard. Early in the series Gavin Thurston captured a stunning shot of her in beautiful morning light as she crept up on a zebra, her body pressed close to the ground, watching until the zebra spooked and raced away. Zawadi promised to keep us on our toes over the next few weeks; seeing her spray-marking prominent rocks, bushes and fallen trees made it abundantly clear to us that she was staking her claim to the area she shared with her mother. Though female relatives often end up sharing parts of the same home range they generally avoid each other as adults: calling and scent-marking lets other leopards know where you are and lessens the chance of conflict.

Finding leopards was always our primary concern. They are nocturnal by nature and, unless they have young cubs, so elusive that it was a blessing still to have Half-Tail and Zawadi to work with. During the rainy season, when the grass grows long and tracks become waterlogged, it was almost impossible to keep track of our leopards: good enough reason not to attempt to film at this time of year.

Youngsters of the Marsh Pride huddled together in the long grass, waiting for their mothers to return and (hopefully) lead them to a kill during the rainy season, when food is sometimes in short supply.

**Pride male**
Scruffy at about six years old. He never developed the large, dark mane typical of many male lions in the Mara. His nose is turning from a youthful pink to black, a sign of age.

This is where having plenty of spotters pays dividends. Using all our resources we managed to locate Half-Tail shortly after we started filming. I could hardly believe our luck. Though Angie and I had known the old female for most of her life, it was a year since we had last seen her. She was tucked away in a patch of dense croton bush some distance to the north of her old home range. As a mother leopard gets older she is often forced to make concessions to her female offspring. With both Beauty and Zawadi needing territories of their own, Half-Tail was being squeezed out, leaving prime areas such as Fig Tree Ridge and Leopard Gorge to her daughters.

Simon was equally excited about the prospect of working with Amber. He had filmed her in the past and was keen to get to know her trio of boisterous cubs – two males and a female – who were nearing independence. The two males were quick and aggressive, always the first to launch an attack, regardless of whether or not they had been seen. As Simon puts it in his commentary: 'They are pioneering with their hunting attempts, if, it has to be said, a little incompetent. But what they lack in technique they make up for in sheer ambition.' Chasing an adult giraffe was certainly aiming a little high, but later in the day we see them lower their sights and take off after a mother wart hog and her piglets. With three cheetahs to contend with, the pig is unable to prevent them from grabbing one of her babies, despite brave attempts to defend them. I had once seen a wart hog knock a leopard off its feet, forcing it to drop the piglet it had snatched from under its mother's nose. But in this instance all the noise created by the battle has alerted a more dangerous enemy still – a lioness. Fortunately by the

time she arrives at the kill the cheetahs have eaten most of it. But rather than slinking away, which would have been the most prudent course of action, they sit and watch the lioness, provoking a charge and chase that are ferocious in their intent and endurance. Even Simon is surprised: 'Rarely have I seen such a concerted effort from a lion to catch and kill a cheetah.'

We had all been waiting for the moment when Amber would leap on to the bonnet of Simon's camera car, hopefully providing our sync crew with the perfect two-shot of presenter and big cat. Intimacy and emotion were what we wanted to convey; in years to come these would define *Big Cat Diary* in people's minds. After all, to us our stars are far more than simply lions, leopards or cheetahs: some of them are like old friends whom we have known for years – from birth to death even – and whom we care about.

From Amber's perspective, of course, it was all about the convenience of having an aerial perch – a warm one at that, early in the morning, with the heat from the engine acting as a hot-water bottle beneath the bonnet. Cheetahs love to take advantage of a high point: they can check the way ahead for danger, look for prey over the long grass and advertise their presence to other cheetahs. They usually choose one of the many termite mounds dotted across the plains for this purpose; it also acts as a convenient latrine. Communicating via these scent posts, they can tell who's around without actually meeting – unless they want to. Like leopards, cheetahs generally tend to avoid one another, spacing themselves across the plains and woodlands as a way of avoiding competition for food and mates.

Amber was at the height of her powers as both mother and huntress, a fact that is eloquently summarised in Simon's narration: 'When stalking she is the embodiment of concentration and stealth. Unlike her cubs Amber is unwilling to launch an attack unless she is confident that the outcome will fall in her favour. The subtle combination of conditions including cover, prey type and mood, light, wind and terrain all play their part in her decision as to whether or not she should launch her blistering attack.' With that Amber races towards camera, head on, straight for the male Thomson's gazelle she has selected. The audience can see that there is no escape from this masterful huntress. A few seconds later she has her victim by the throat, a forepaw stretched across its belly to prevent it from getting to its feet.

Amber was at this time 11 years of age, old by wild cheetah standards. The same was true of Half-Tail, and each time we found her I couldn't help reminding myself that I might never see her again. Leopards must draw on all their guile and experience to survive amongst the lions and hyenas in the Mara and although there are records of them living for 12 or more years (there is a female leopard in Londolozi Game Reserve in South Africa who is 17), this is unusual. How they die we can usually only guess at, but lions are certainly one of the greatest threats, as we were about to witness.

One evening, while searching for Half-Tail, we hear jackals barking in alarm, alerting us to the place where she has just killed a hare. Two lionesses have also heard the high-pitched yelps and have come to investigate.

Right: Two of Amber's adolescent cubs perched on a spotter's car. The rough tread of the spare wheel makes it easy for them to grip.

Half-Tail and Zawadi in October 1996, when Zawadi was about nine months old. A leopard is always cautious when she has cubs, constantly stopping and looking for signs of danger.

I watch with a mixture of fascination and horror as the lions blindside Half-Tail, stalking towards her with such intent that it makes the hair stand up on the back of my neck – they are looking to kill her. At the last minute Half-Tail sees them and, with a deep, explosive grunt, turns and races for the safety of a massive fig tree, hare firmly clasped in her mouth. Documentary cameraman Richard North, one of whose specialities is tracking golf balls flying through the air, nearly rips his camera from its mount as he struggles to keep Half-Tail in frame, recording the whole event.

All I can manage is a rather feeble 'That is about the closest call I've seen Half-Tail make', but far from being shaken by the incident she acts almost as if nothing has happened. For her it is all part of day-to-day living. The same is true for all of our cats. The world is full of dangers, eventualities to be dealt with as they happen, then straight back to the priorities in life – eating, mating, rearing cubs. Whenever danger does intrude on their lives the 'fight and flight' response kicks in, sending a surge of adrenalin through their system, readying them to respond instantly to challenges such as this. While Half-Tail's pupils are still widely dilated and her ears set back, once she is safely ensconced in the top of the fig tree all our wily old leopard is interested in doing is polishing off her meal as quickly as possible, leaving the lionesses staring up at her in frustration. While humans may sometimes be paralysed by the fear of what might lie in wait for them in the future, the big cats simply get on with life.

**No pushover – even for lions**
Buffalo are an important prey species for lions in the Mara, particularly when the migration has departed. But they are formidable creatures, with bulls such as this not uncommonly weighing up to 750 kg (1650 lb).

Having said this, there was plenty of excitement in store for the Marsh Lions. This series will always be remembered for their dramatic encounter with the herd of buffaloes that every so often swept through the Bila Shaka lugga, the nursery area for the pride's young cubs. The power play between lions and buffaloes is the ultimate spectacle. Lions attempting to pull down one of these huge creatures is normally a battle of epic proportions, frightening in its intensity but riveting to watch.

Up until this point the Marsh Lions had provided us with hours of wonderful viewing as they nurtured their young cubs. Recently three more had been introduced to the pride, making 11 in total, all under three months old. We had watched as the mother gently carried her young in her mouth to a new den site; waited for the lionesses to lead the cubs to their first kill; and sat spellbound as they took their first tentative steps towards their male relatives Scruffy and Scar, prompting their mothers to quickly block their path until they were certain that the youngsters would come to no harm.

Two weeks earlier the Marsh Pride had had their first run-in with the buffaloes, though on that occasion both sides retreated, the honours even. But this time the buffaloes were back with a vengeance. What happened next was one of the most harrowing incidents I have ever witnessed. In the dry season the Bila Shaka lugga provides the herd with scattered pools of water where they can drink. The Marsh Pride know this and sometimes over the years they have lain in ambush. During the drought of 1993 the lugga provided easy killing for the lions; the normally fearsome buffaloes were so weak that they offered little resistance and soon the area was littered with carcasses. For some time afterwards the Marsh Lions targeted buffaloes, having learned how best to tackle them. At least one of the lionesses I was now watching had been barely a year old in 1993, but had been able to practise her hunting skills on the stricken animals. Now the tables were turned, and she was desperately trying to protect her cubs.

It is the noise that I remember most, the lionesses' deep, rumbles of threat and fear, mixed with the grunts and throaty clicks of the buffaloes as they try to destroy the cubs. The buffaloes have smelt the lions among the croton thickets – now they can see them. They thunder forward, scattering the cats in all directions. The lionesses try to divert the onrush – they have seen this all before – attempting to draw the bulls away as the cubs panic and run into the open, terrified. From the buffaloes' point of view this is all about 'mobbing' the lions, trying to force them to move on so they can eat and drink in peace. Killing lion cubs – even adults at times – helps to underline to even the most powerful of predators that buffaloes are not to be trifled with: a potent form of anti-predator behaviour.

A buffalo attack is brutally direct – they charge, lowering their head with neck muscles bulging as they slam into their opponent, hooking at it with heavy curved horns. Watching them, I am stunned by the sheer brute strength of the bulls as they trample and thrash the bushes, determined to root out the cubs. I have been chased by buffaloes; now I have a far clearer idea of what might happen next. Some people say you should lie down if you are charged, but unless there is a convenient tree to escape up you are done for, repeatedly trampled and horned. As we film I have glimpses of cubs scurrying through the long grass, see bulls pile-driving the spot where the little cats have been, and think that this is surely the end for most of them. The hero of the hour is Scruffy, who repeatedly returns to the fray, risking his life in his attempts to prevent the bulls from killing the cubs. Scar is far more circumspect (to put it politely), reluctant to get involved and intent more on his own safety than on that of the cubs, a character trait that we would witness again in the years to come.

Lion cubs love to play when it has been raining – all that mud and water make the perfect setting for fun and games. The cub between its mother's legs is Moja, whom we followed in 2005 (see Chapter 7).

Watching the programme, you can see how shaken I am: 'I've never seen anything like this in my life and having watched this group with their tiny cubs it's incredibly distressing. We started with 11 cubs and to be honest I haven't got a clue how many are left, the lionesses certainly don't know, they're moving around calling, calling, calling, desperately looking for their little cubs. The way those buffaloes were just hammering into the grass I would be amazed if there aren't some dead cubs round here.'

For my own benefit as much as for the audience,

I try to make sense of what I have just seen: 'Watching lionesses with little cubs like that, you feel almost responsible for them and when a bunch of buffaloes come in and act like the heavies the first thing you feel like doing is driving them away. But there is no way you can do that. You can't play favourites in circumstances like that and I always try and remind myself how many buffalo calves have been killed by lions.'

In the end only one of the cubs perished. After gently licking its little body the mother ate it,

recouping some of her investment in its life. Writing about his time studying lions in the Serengeti, the American zoologist George Schaller put this kind of incident into perspective: 'I was not sure what to expect, certainly not a wild expression of grief, but perhaps some sentiment. Instead she ate the cub, and as I sat there listening to her crunch the bones of her offspring, I could only conclude that it is difficult for man to return in imagination to the simplicity of a lion's outlook.'

But it wasn't all doom and gloom. One of the

most satisfying moments of the series for me was when Zawadi decided to stalk a hare right in front of my vehicle. It was one of those days when everything falls into place. Richard North was set up in the back hatch ready to film a sync piece with me, with Zawadi beautifully framed in the background – a perfect two-shot. Like most big cats, leopards spend 80 per cent or more of their time resting or sleeping, but the younger ones such as Zawadi quite often move around during the day, hunting smaller prey. On this occasion our leopard suddenly metamorphoses from relaxed cat to stalking predator. The change is instantaneous, and you can imagine how exciting and energising moments like these are when you have been sitting in your vehicle all day.

With her pin-sharp eyes Zawadi has spotted the hare crouched among the tangle of long grass and fallen acacia bushes. She creeps forward in a wide arc, making not a sound as she places each paw carefully on the ground, closing in behind her prey. When she is within striking distance she pauses, gathers herself, then springs high in the air like a serval cat, snagging the hare with her dew claw – the razor-sharp claw on her wrist – before it can escape. The hare utters a cry of distress, silenced instantly by a bite to the back of its neck. But that single sound is enough to bring a hyena running to investigate, prompting Zawadi to launch herself into the top of a spindly acacia bush. 'Nothing's too small for a leopard,' I observe. 'It's probably one of the reasons there are actually more leopards than lions and cheetahs on this planet, because they have to be the most adaptable of all the cats – they can take anything from a lizard to a hare such as this, right up to a large antelope – and I mean the speed!'

When I watch that piece of footage it all looks seamless: I manage to say something sensible while Richard shoots the scene so beautifully, widening the image at just the right moment to capture the hyena rushing in, that it barely needs editing. And the star of course is Zawadi, who performs to perfection and earns a tasty snack for herself in the process.

Even though Amber's cubs were nearly a year and a half old – around the age that cheetahs become independent – they still lacked experience. As Simon comments during one particular hunt, 'In fact, just when we thought that Amber's cubs had life sorted, they've been illustrating how truly naive they still are regarding the more challenging situations they find themselves in – hunting a newborn topi calf may not appear to be much of a problem for the fastest animals on earth, but what Amber's cubs haven't taken into account is that the topi mother is big, powerful, with sharp horns and backed up by the bulls in the herd.' With Amber there to draw the topi mother away, the cubs do manage to secure their kill. They feed quickly and quietly so as not to alert lions or hyenas to their presence, but as Simon cautions, 'If the family does split soon they're in for a very sudden reality check.'

Sure enough, when Simon next locates the three young cheetahs they are on their own. The reassuring presence of their mother is gone and the youngsters face a difficult time.

Opposite: Cheetah cubs start to follow their mother when they are six to eight weeks old, allowing her to range more widely.

Right: A cheetah's head is perfectly designed for hunting – large forward-facing eyes and flat face improve binocular vision, the flat head helps to conceal the cheetah when stalking, and the large nostrils maximise the intake of oxygen when sprinting after prey.

The stories we feature on *Big Cat Diary* work best when they create a real sense of 'jeopardy' – a word with which we would become all too familiar later in the series' history, meaning that our stars themselves are in danger. And that is certainly the case now.

The cubs act nervously, staying in the same place and constantly looking around them, jumping at their own shadows. Occasionally they call, uttering that distinctive, high-pitched, whistle-like yelp that carries far across the plains: they must hope it will alert their mother to their whereabouts. But even if she hears their distressed contact call, it will go unheeded – by now Amber is almost certainly pregnant with her next litter.

The arrival of the migration signals the good times for all the big cats. The herds' favoured river-crossing sites make for easy killing.

Simon watches over the cubs like a surrogate mother as they weigh up their options: 'This is where all the months of training will be put to the test. Past experience tells us that though they have the speed and the power to subdue prey, they often fail in the decision-making. If Amber were with them she would go for the Thomson's gazelle baby.' Fortunately they make the right choice:

'An impressive start, perhaps, but this is only the beginning of a very steep learning curve.' When jackals arrive, the young cheetahs show their inexperience yet again, taking time out to chase them away (a fruitless waste of energy) instead of feeding as quickly as they can.

Zawadi is also still showing her youthful side. In one sequence when she spots a potential prey she is suddenly all business, crawling on her belly, head low, her eyes on food. Then mid-way through her careful approach she pauses and rolls onto her back, legs in the air, prompting me to remark that 'hidden within that adult body is still the playful cub of two years ago'. It is not uncommon to see a cat suddenly stopped in its tracks by an interesting scent – of another

leopard, perhaps, or the droppings of a herbivore – then rolling sinuously in the pungent odour. Some people have surmised that this might mask a predator's own scent, helping it to stalk prey undetected, but it seems more likely that the smell stimulates the cat in a sexual way, like cat-nip. It certainly looks to be a pleasant experience, however messy.

Wonderful as it is to be able to find a leopard, even if it is resting peacefully in a tree, I remark at one point, 'When you do, you can pretty much guarantee there's going to be lots of sitting around and waiting. Zawadi can do that because her diet is so rich in protein. But if prey were to pass though this area and she had her eyes open she would be down that tree like a shot.' Aidan

Woodward, one of our leopard spotters, had cottoned on to the fact that Zawadi liked to rest up in trees; if by the middle of the morning we had failed to find her he would start to search all the likely trees in the area where she had last been seen on the chance that he would pick out a spotted tail or dark silhouette against the skyline. And quite often he did.

Weaving their way through our story were the great herds of wildebeest and zebra. When living in the Mara I always tend to measure time by the arrival and departure of 'the migration' – a collective term embracing the 1.5 million wildebeest and more than 200,000 zebras that roam the Mara–Serengeti ecosystem, an area of more than 25,000 sq. km (10,000 sq. miles). These herbivores sweep everything before them as they surge into the reserve, knocking down the grass like a giant lawnmower: wherever you look the plains are blackened by their presence. And when the herds decide to cross the Mara River it is one of the great wildlife spectacles on earth – the sound of wildebeest grunting and croaking like an army of frogs, the zebras braying like dogs as family members try to stay in contact among the press of animals, is simply deafening.

There is a poignancy to the crossings, too. When the river is swollen, hundreds of wildebeest are crushed and trampled underfoot, their bodies washed downstream, food for the crocodiles and vultures, catfish and monitor lizards. 'For some exhausted youngsters there is a swift conclusion to their journey,' comments Simon as a calf staggers, stunned by a glancing blow from the head of a massive crocodile. A second blow knocks it to its knees, crouched like a gallant prize-fighter too bewildered to regain his feet. The crocodile lashes out a third time, grabbing the calf's spindly leg in its gin-trap of a mouth, then sinks beneath the surface, dragging the calf to its death.

Many wildebeest calves are separated from their mother in the confusion of these crossings. Cows and calves run backwards and forwards, calling urgently. 'One young calf hears its mother's voice on the near side and decides, though exhausted, to make the final supreme effort to recross the turbid waters. Though it may appear folly or ignorance to us, the instinctive draw of its mother's call dictates its course of action.' On this occasion the crocodiles are too sated to pursue the calf and there is a good chance that it did meet up with its mother.

**B**ut as always it was the stories of the big cats that held our interest most intently. We all felt an insatiable desire to know what happened next. Much to our astonishment Amber's cubs were reunited with their mother – a unique moment captured by our cameras. And my old friend Half-Tail had a trick or two up her sleeve as well. It transpired that she had given birth to two more cubs, a male and a female, a few months before we started filming and, though they were shy and we caught only glimpses of them throughout the series, it was enough. At one point Half-Tail struggles to carry a half-eaten impala kill into a tree as the light fades, only to fall to the ground, nearly crushing the bolder of the cubs under the carcass. On another occasion, we find her suckling among the cover of a thorn-choked lugga. 'This is what makes it all worthwhile,' I remark. 'I've spent weeks, months, years trying to track down leopards, happy initially just for the sight of a spotted coat disappearing into the long grass. But this, the sight of a mother leopard and a small cub – intimate moments – is as good as it gets.' Little did I realise that this would be one of the last times I saw Half-Tail and her cubs. But that is to get ahead of our story…

Against all our predictions, Amber and her family are still together as the credits roll for the last time. With such a good mother, the young cheetahs have been given a fantastic start in life and their future looks very bright indeed. Simon rounds out a remarkable series: 'They have provided us with moments of beauty, drama, intimacy and joy in the most stunning of African wild places. Though our time here has come to a close, the world of the big cat is timeless.' His words are played over a montage of stunning images of dawn and dusk, of our big cats in action, moments of tenderness and pure savagery.

It is this extraordinary mix of imagery, music and commentary that will see us back in the Mara in the autumn of 2000.

bigcat diary

SERIES 3
2000

King of
Beasts

Series 3 opens with Simon hanging on for dear life in the back of David Breed's camera car as they race across the plains. He wipes a bead of sweat from his brow as he explains our mission: 'We've just heard that a lion has started to hunt some wildebeest and we're still some way off and can only hope that we can get there in time.' This is very much the reality of life in the bush, whether you happen to be working on *Big Cat Diary* or earning your living as a wildlife photographer. You always want to be where the action is, but as often as not you arrive after the event or miss the shot. The only way to beat the system is to spend weeks at a time in pursuit of your quarry; you have to live the experience day in, day out. And as of August 2000 that is what the *Big Cat* team would be doing for the next two months.

I walk into view along the flank of Rhino Ridge, my outline distorted by the heat haze: 'So what's different about the Mara this year? Well, for a start it's the worst drought in living memory. I've never seen anything like it. That is going to make life tough for most of our animals, but for our big cats it's going to be a feast.' I had witnessed a number of devastating droughts over the years, such as the one that hit the Mara with the force of a sledge hammer when the short rains failed in 1993. The Masai's cattle died in their hundreds, so did the hippos, and the buffalo population crashed by 80 per cent to fewer than 3,000 animals.

For visitors, though, the 2000 drought proved a blessing, ensuring that hundreds of thousands of wildebeest and zebras poured into the Mara from the Serengeti to the south. Our cameramen captured stunning backlit views as a million cloven hoofs kicked up spumes of dust and the herds headed across the lifeless plains in search of greener pastures.

The Blonde Males searching for Kali's cubs along the Bila Shaka Lugga. They have picked up the scent of mother and cubs but on this occasion were unable to find them.

Simon sets up the series with a reprise of the events of two years earlier, particularly the buffaloes' assault on the Marsh Pride's cubs: 'But despite facing seemingly impossible odds, at least eight of those cubs have survived and now they are fit and rather typical adolescents. Though they may look laid back and relaxed they've experienced a bit of a family upheaval recently and been pushed out of their traditional home by two adult males who look like they have every intention of taking over the territory.'

The two males in question were from the Topi Plains Pride. Angie and I had watched them earlier in the year as they made their first tentative forays into Marsh Pride territory. The door had been opened for them by the death of Scruffy, killed by Masai herdsmen a few months earlier in reprisal for a cattle-stealing incident. This left Scar on his own – a vulnerable position for a pride male. Shortly afterwards the herdsmen also killed two of the Marsh Lionesses, reducing to just three the five adult lionesses we had filmed in 1998 and seriously weakening the pride's ability to defend its territory.

We watched as these two impressive Blonde Males attempted to intimidate the Marsh Pride females early one morning along the Bila Shaka lugga. On this occasion they were soundly rebuffed, but this was to prove no more than a temporary setback, a recce to test the strength and resolve of the pride – and to see if there were any young cubs. If there were, they would seek to kill them.

One of the Blonde Males was older and larger that the other and he led the way when the pair returned a few days later. They scoured the lugga

Kali with two of her cubs. You can see the intent look on her face as she watches the Blonde Males moving along the lugga.

for signs of the Marsh Pride, sniffing and scent-marking the bushes, a look of deadly earnest on their battle-scarred faces. But the lionesses had wisely headed for the marsh – all except the oldest, Kali, who had recently given birth to four cubs, sired four months earlier by Scar. The males could smell the cubs' scent, but failed to find them: somehow Kali and her tiny offspring managed to escape, creeping away through the long grass. A day or so later Scar was forced to run for his life as the Blonde Males pursued him across the plains, roaring as they went. On and on they ran, all the way to the Musiara Gate at the northern edge of the Marsh Pride's territory. Satisfied, the Blonde Males turned and headed back to the place they now considered their second home.

For a while the Blonde Males continued to consort with the Topi Plains females and the year-old-cubs they had fathered, dividing their time between that pride and the Bila Shaka Lugga, which Scruffy and Scar's two-year-old sons had also deserted, fleeing to the marsh with their female relatives. Kali's young cubs soon perished, almost certainly killed by the Blonde Males. By ousting the adolescents and killing

the cubs, the new males were soon able to mate with their mothers, including Kali.

The marsh is a prime hunting ground during the dry season and never more so than when vast numbers of wildebeest, zebras and buffaloes are drawn to this oasis of food and water. Over the next few weeks the young outcasts from the Marsh Pride would have plenty of opportunity to practise their fledgling hunting skills. The muddy surrounds provided the perfect ambush site, as well as a cool retreat from the burning sun. While this suited the lions, it often proved a death trap for their prey and with the advantage of numbers to counter their inexperience the killing proved easy; even the two bumbling young males met with success on occasion. Once in a while a wildebeest would turn and defend itself with its sharply curved horns, forcing the young lions to back off long enough for it to escape, though more often than not, with half a dozen robust adolescent lions to contend with, any form of

defence proved futile. Even creatures the size of a hippo were irresistible to our youngsters, providing Simon and the lion crew with plenty of high-octane action – even Scar decided to join in the fray at one point, though not for long. You can see the frustration on Simon's face, hear it in his voice, when the sudden appearance of some Masai puts paid to an extraordinary encounter. The lions move off into cover, leaving the mortally wounded hippo to suffer a lingering death along the river bank.

Despite the drought, we were sometimes besieged by afternoon thunderstorms and heavy downpours, making it all too easy for our vehicles to get stuck and difficult for us to film. My heavy old Toyota LandCruiser, which was already causing me much grief and embarrassment from the number of punctures I was having crisscrossing the acacia woodlands favoured by our leopards, now came in for a good deal of ribbing. But heavy is comfortable, and with a stash of macadamias, cashew nuts and other selected goodies tucked away in the wooden cupboards my safari wagon proved a popular venue for a snack or a game drive!

# big Cat diary

## Leopard
## fact file...

### Who's who?
The spots and rosettes on a leopard's face and coat are the most reliable guide to identification. This is Zawadi.

### Out of harm's way
Climbing trees is a leopard's safest way of escaping from predators such as lions and hyenas.

### A leopard's tail
Like cheetahs, leopards use their tails for balance. The white underside also gives cubs a 'flag' to follow.

# The story of Half-Tail

**M**uch had happened during the two years since our last series, not least the death of Half-Tail, whose story I had narrated in a *Big Cat* update filmed in 1999. Watching a montage of highlights from past programmes at the top of the latest series reminded me just how much I had loved following this extraordinary leopard. To summarise what had been happening I recorded a piece to camera while walking along the edge of the Mara River, close to the place where I had last seen Half-Tail: Simon and I were always looking for opportunities to mix things up a bit when it came to presenting, taking any excuse we could to get out of our vehicles, wherever this was permitted.

Half-Tail was 11 or 12 years old when she finally disappeared in March 1999. Word was that she had run into trouble with Masai herdsmen after worming her way through a temporary thornbush enclosure to snatch a goat or a sheep; when she returned a second time to the same place the herdsmen were ready with a wire snare anchored to a log. By now Half-Tail was famous, with a following around the world, and people were naturally reluctant to talk for fear of trouble – herdsmen are expected to notify the authorities about predator/livestock incidents so they can take appropriate action, killing or trapping the culprit. Though it is legal to kill a predator who threatens your life or livelihood, the authorities would have

expected Half-Tail's death to be reported to them.

With the help of our old friend William Kipen, who had driven Simon's camera vehicle during the first series, we began to piece together the story of her demise. Later still our cheetah cameraman Warren Samuels, who had camped for many years along the Mara River bordering Half-Tail's territory, added some more information that only deepened the mystery. He had been told by a colleague that Half-Tail had somehow managed to break free from the snare – perhaps she had chewed through the wire. Apparently she then sought refuge in a tree but slipped or became tangled and hanged herself with the wire pulled tight around her neck. Her body was then thrown into the Mara River. Who knows the truth; it was certainly a tragic end for an extraordinary cat. To the herdsmen, of course, she was the enemy, 'the goat killer' and a thief. Half-Tail had crossed the line, broken the pact by which the Masai are prepared to live side by side with wild animals. If the big cats keep a low profile and refrain from stealing livestock, then the herdsmen can co-exist with them. If not, they must pay the price, which under the circumstances seems only fair.

Top: Half-Tail before she lost her tail, which may have happened in a scrap with baboons or in a fight over territory with another female.

Above: Half-Tail's legacy: this little female (underneath) was killed by a lioness, but her brother Mang'aa survived to become a beautiful adult male.

Although Half-Tail has gone, her legacy lives
on. Zawadi was proof of that, and by 2000 she
had a cub of her own – a young female called Safi.
Angie and I had watched Zawadi with two small
cubs on Fig Tree Ridge at the dawn of the new
millennium. A few months later Safi's boisterous
twin brother had been killed by lions. He was six
months old. Now was my chance to catch up with
the little female, who was nearly eleven months
but still quite a bit smaller than her mother. Our
spotters had located Zawadi resting in a tree with
a kill, as relaxed and calm as you could hope for:
'It's as if we weren't even here.'

The leopard crew stayed with Zawadi all day;
once you've found a leopard you never leave her.
Anxious for her to become active before it was too
dark to film, Warwick Sloss already had his camera
ramped up to maximum 'gain' or light-gathering
capability. My heart starts to pound as Safi appears
out of the darkness. She seems nervous,
approaching only so far before calling to Zawadi
for a sign that it is safe to move closer. Zawadi
grunts in acknowledgement and begins her descent
silhouetted amid the tapestry of branches, coal
black against the fading sky, all feline elegance:
our hours of waiting have paid off. Mother and
cub greet briefly before Safi climbs into the tree
to feed alone in the manner leopards like best.

When we cut to the cheetahs, it is Simon's turn
to exult in the company of an old friend. He checks
the female's face markings through his binoculars,
looking for two distinctive lines of spots on the right
cheek. And sure enough: 'It's Amber.' Last time he
had seen her she had been accompanied by three
almost fully grown offspring and as far as we knew
she had failed to raise any cubs since then. Life is
very different for a cheetah without cubs and
though Simon thought that Amber might be
pregnant he was keen to have a Plan B; a female
without cubs means lots of daylight hunting but not
much else. So when our spotters located the male
territory-holder Kimbia, Simon decided to focus
on him as well, to try to reveal the different lifestyles

Zawadi drinking. The intermittent watercourses or luggas are very important for a mother leopard – she can hide her cubs among the croton and acacia thickets, and find water to drink, particularly when she is lactating.

followed by male and female cheetahs.

With the migration in full spate, Kimbia is quick to respond to the opportunity of a sizeable meal: 'Cheetahs are the most specialised of the big cats, trimmed to the max for speed, but their streamlined form means they lack power compared to lions or leopards – a wildebeest is a real challenge both in terms of speed and strength.' As Simon speaks these words, Kimbia races after a young wildebeest, struggling to overpower it before bringing it crashing to the ground. The action is accompanied by Warren's driver Wilson Wemali's animated Swahili commentary, which has such energy that it really doesn't matter that the audience can't understand a word he is saying. Sitting all day in a vehicle waiting for the cats to do something can be wearing for the most patient of souls, so the moments when it finally comes together are worth celebrating.

Safi at three months looking warily around for hyenas

Even at this age Safi's brother (left) was larger than she was

57

A cheetah male can consume around 14 kg (30 lb) of meat at a sitting on an empty stomach, so Kimbia was able to feast until his belly swelled like a balloon. The problem was that over the next few weeks he spent most of his time doing absolutely nothing besides marking the occasional tree with a pungent mix of urine and anal gland secretions, leaving his calling card for other cheetahs passing through the area.

Kimbia had tracked down Amber's daughter, whom we had featured in the last series when she was still with her mother and two brothers. After the family split up the three youngsters stayed together for another few months, co-operating in their hunting and in defending their kills. But once the female was ready to become sexually active she abandoned her siblings and began to live the solitary life that is the norm for female cheetahs, except when they have cubs.

The aggressive spat that ensued when Kimbia charged towards Amber's daughter along Rhino Ridge was just the kind of thing we had been hoping to record. As the young female yelps in appeasement, Kimbia repeatedly leaps high in the air above her, growling aggressively, intimidating her and prompting her to pee in fear. This is just what he wants, allowing him the chance to investigate her scent for signs of oestrus, possibly even helping to initiate the process of bringing her into season.

From Rhino Ridge you have a perfect view over Paradise Plain, where the wildebeest now gathered. The herds' presence gives a special kind of energy to living in the Mara in the dry season. Our camera crews took every opportunity to record the spectacle, capturing glorious scenes of column after column of wildebeest crisscrossing the dusty plains. We also filmed an epic river crossing at the point where Paradise Plain borders the Mara River. I had photographed a similar event there 25 years earlier with Keith Scholey; the contours of the banks of the river had changed but the dust and noise were as powerfully evocative as ever.

Meanwhile Simon watched as more animals crossed the river opposite Kichwa Tembo Camp, tracking their journey as they made their way down to the marsh. Here the Marsh Pride was in total disarray, allowing a succession of other lions – nomads and pride members from adjacent territories – the chance to encroach. But this seemed to make little difference to Scar, who had somehow survived the takeover of his territory. In fact by staying close to his younger relatives he was prospering – at about eight years old he was still in his prime and had only been forced to abandon his territory when he lost his pride mate Scruffy. There are lovely scenes of him being greeted solicitously by the two

The wildebeest and zebra migration is one of nature's great spectacles and one of the reasons we film *Big Cat Diary* during the dry season. At this time up to 600,000 wildebeest and tens of thousands of zebras flood into the Mara from the Serengeti in search of fresh grazing and water.

adolescent males and, whenever the youngsters killed, Scar would invariably take the lion's share. As Simon reflects, 'While all the adolescents are looking quite skinny he however is the size of a house.' To underline this statement one of the youngsters then pulls down a zebra foal at dusk, only to have Scar immediately appropriate the kill for himself.

The pride was now under pressure on two separate fronts. While the Topi Plains males had commandeered the Bila Shaka area, the Ridge Pride had invaded from the south, capitalising on the hunting opportunities presented by the wildebeest that had moved into the area. 'They were certainly a force to be reckoned with, 21 lions in all: two adult males, six lionesses and 13 youngsters, including one tiny cub whom we named Solo – the only survivor of a litter born to the oldest lioness in the pride.' We were to see a lot more of Solo as the weeks went by. He was the most adorable little cub, and everyone at our base camp wanted to come out and see him. His year-old relatives thought he was adorable too, endlessly playing with him: and though the play occasionally looked rough Solo seemed to love all the attention – most of the time. The tenacity and toughness he showed were inspiring; with no siblings of his own age he would need every bit of luck if he was to survive.

By now *Big Cat Diary* was beginning to become a brand with an online presence, and at the end of each programme the audience was invited to find out more about our big cats on the Nature Website. We were keen to blend a more informal style of presenting as well as including glimpses behind the scenes. With this in mind Simon introduced the second programme from camp, giving the audience an insight into how we operate: 'In *Big Cat Diary* the cats are of course the stars, but they don't just wait for us to turn up. They're always posing new sorts of problems every single day. This is our base camp and it is from here that we set out to try and find those cats. Jonathan and I are backed up by an incredibly experienced team of seven camera crews and at least eight different spotters.' Cue music, dust and a convoy of vehicles heading down the road in the direction of where we had left our lions, leopards and cheetahs the previous night. Radios were crucial to the whole operation, allowing us to keep track of what everyone was doing. A repeater tower was erected 300 m (1,000 ft) above the plains along the top of the Siria Escarpment to help ensure that all of the teams could communicate with base camp in the event of an emergency or exciting news about our cats that needed relaying.

Watching Series 3, I can feel a transformation taking place. Simon and I are trying to be more relaxed with the audience while still remaining informative. Wherever possible we film pieces to camera outside our vehicles, underlining the fact that talking from the interior of the car made for a rather static presentation. Our camera operators constantly try to dream up new and exciting viewpoints with their super-wide-angle lenses and mini-cams mounted on an extendable pole. The pole cam is great for filming cheetah cubs crawling around under the car, but when it is turned on us it has the potential to make us look like cartoon figures: one image shot through the roof hatch has me looking like Noddy driving a bus, with a tiny steering wheel straight out of Toy Town; funnier still is the mini-camera clamped to my mirror which transforms me into some kind of crazed mustang with nostrils the size of golf balls and rodent-like incisors. The editors love it, of course, and it makes for great comedy moments – but only in the programmes you never see.

**Right:** I am a legend in the Mara – there is nowhere I have not found a large hole to disappear into or a rock to smash one of my shock absorbers.
**Left:** Cheetah brothers stay together for life. A powerful coalition such as Honey's Boys (see Chapter 9) will dominate an area, ranging widely and injuring or even killing single males they catch intruding on their territory.

Lions in the Mara grow up
in the presence of safari vehicles

61

# bigCat diary

## When do we eat?

For all of us, long days incarcerated in stiflingly hot safari wagons were tempered by the prospect of food. Initially this arrived packed in regulation white cardboard containing a hotch-potch of sandwiches and fruit with a couple of sausages and some bacon thrown in for good measure. By the middle of the day a pile of soggy pineapple-soaked sandwiches and sweaty pieces of quiche looked pretty unappetising, until Angie was co-opted into co-ordinating the team's picnics with the chefs at Governor's Camp. By the following year we would each have our own cool bag filled with plastic containers stuffed with all kinds of goodies from yogurts to muffins, as well as salads and thermoses of hot food and soup, bringing a smile to everyone's faces. The *pièce de résistance* was offerings from our camp manager and professional hunter Collin Wellensky's vegetable garden at Governor's – if you wanted rocket and herbs it was best to be at the picnic table early. When I had time I started preparing my lunch during breakfast, – but when things were busy and the cats were performing then we might skip breakfast all together or combine it with lunch.

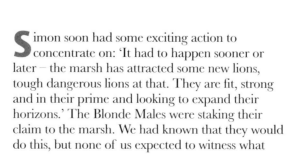

Simon soon had some exciting action to concentrate on: 'It had to happen sooner or later – the marsh has attracted some new lions, tough dangerous lions at that. They are fit, strong and in their prime and looking to expand their horizons.' The Blonde Males were staking their claim to the marsh. We had known that they would do this, but none of us expected to witness what

happened next. As the two lions plunge through the marsh dripping with mud, the local hyena clan moves in to challenge them. Up until now the hyenas have fronted up to the youngsters from the Marsh Pride with a degree of success, sometimes even forcing them from their kill. But adult male lions are a different proposition.

We have already seen how treacherous the

**Opposite:** A Marsh Lioness greets one of the pride males. A female will solicit mating opportunities when she is in season.
**Left:** The older Blonde Male mating with Mama Lugga (see Chapter 4). Lions mate repeatedly over a period of up to a week, with an average of three to four cubs born three and a half months later.

marsh can be underfoot, but the hyenas are determined to intimidate the new arrivals, tails flared, whooping and wailing as they close in. The Blonde Males are having none of it: 'These two males want to make it absolutely clear who is boss.' The larger lion spots a lone hyena loping away through the reeds and immediately gives chase, showing a frightening turn of speed as he bounds after the terrified animal who howls in fear, mouth agape in appeasement. What follows is shocking in its violence; the two males tear into their victim, ignoring the cries of protest from the other members of the clan who vainly try to drive the lions away with a barrage of sound. Finally the older male makes a deep, fatal bite into the hyena's neck.

Simon tries to make sense of the scene for the audience: 'This is a statement, a clear signal to all the hyenas and any lion onlookers that these males mean business. It may look extreme to our eyes, but it is what these guys are built for and precisely what the young males in the marsh have been unable to do.' The new males immediately start to strut around as if they own the place – and of course they do – scuffing their feet, marking the area with their scent. 'This does not look good for our young lions, especially the males, who won't be welcome here. Scar, their father, is typically nowhere to be seen. Some of the young females are, however, intrigued: they are torn between caution and curiosity – after all, these fit males could be just what they are looking for to help defend cubs in the future; as far as fidelity in lion society is concerned it just depends on who is toughest.' Hopefully in two years' time we would find the Marsh Pride with well-established males and plenty of cubs to film.

This page: Kimbia, the dominant male cheetah in the area at this time, in a spat with Amber's daughter. This sort of contact may help bring a female into season, allowing the male to mate.
Opposite: Amber's daughter. When female cheetahs become independent they usually overlap part of their mother's home range. They do not defend this area as males do – they simply avoid other adult females.

Meanwhile, Zawadi and Safi had disappeared. Our leopard spotter Aidan had been given a hand-held digital video camera in case something happened before we could reach him. As luck would have it he captured some exciting footage of Zawadi fighting with a male leopard, who was distinguished by a damaged lower jaw, to prevent him from harming Safi. Male leopards, like lions, will kill cubs sired by previous territory-holders so that they can mate with the mother. Safi was nearly a year old and spending long periods on her own, but the male was still potentially a threat and Zawadi was taking no chances, lashing out and harassing him, using her body to block his path and driving him away. The following day we could find

no sign of our two leopards and it seemed likely that they had moved to a safer area. But where?

We spent the next two weeks scouring every corner of Zawadi's territory and beyond, and at one point we did find a mother leopard with a six-month-old cub feasting on a Thomson's gazelle kill in a giant fig tree along the Talek River: it was tempting to focus on them, but as I said at the time, 'I know I'd have little chance keeping track of these leopards. As soon as they'd finished their kill I'd be starting from scratch with leopards I know nothing about.' But in years to come we would be only too happy to spend time with Bella and her daughter Olive, who were destined to become stars of *Big Cat* in their own right.

A massive storm threatens overhead, heralding the end of the drought and providing a suitably dramatic conclusion to the series. Simon sums up his feelings for Amber: 'Maybe it is just because I have known her now for more than seven years, seen her raise a family, watched her struggle through the lean times; she's somehow a step above the rest, a real queen among cats. We named her after the colour of her eyes and once you've gazed into them at close quarters you are absolutely captivated, caught in her spell.' At this point Amber jumps up onto the bonnet of Simon's car one more time and he says, 'I'm really glad we caught up with her. This may be one of the last times we get to see her.'

He was right. At some point early the following year Amber vanished. As is so often the case, none of us know what happened to her: disease, a violent end perhaps. Death on the African plain is rarely a peaceful event. One slip, one false move, a slight miscalculation and you pay for it with your life.

For a few moments we cut away from the big cats and glory in beautiful wide views of the Mara: elephants at sunrise, then a reprise of some of the best moments we have witnessed with our cats over the past two months, moments of high drama and beauty. But there is still one story holding the audience in thrall. Solo and his mother have gone missing. One of our lion spotters, Peter Blackwell, manages to locate the mother as she heads south of Rhino Ridge, calling. Her face is bloody as if she has been feeding – or fighting; apparently the Ridge Pride have got into a scrap with other lions during the night. I comment, 'The way she is looking says it all as far as I'm concerned. Solo's gone.'

We all felt gutted. Solo had captivated us with his enduring spirit. We had watched as his mother carefully nurtured him, laughed with joy as he played with her, stayed with her as she recovered from a beating from members of a neighbouring pride early on in the series, leaving her so badly wounded that she could barely lie down.

We called in all our spotters to help in the search and a short while later Pete was back on the radio to say they had found Solo looking lost and lonely. At least he was alive, though his mum was wandering around 3 km (2 miles) away. At one point as we film the little cub starts to panic and walks out into the open. It is essential that he seeks cover and buries himself in the undergrowth. If jackals or hyenas find him that will be the end of it. We all hold our breath and hope for a happy conclusion – there is no way we can just pick Solo up and reunite him with his mother.

After what seems like an eternity, Solo's mum turns and heads in the direction of where the little cub is crouched in the grass. She stops every so often, stares, calls, then listens, until finally she puts us out of our misery and is reunited with her cub. She bends down to greet him – he looks so tiny – and they lie in the long grass, licking and grooming, the little cub batting playfully at his mother's face. These are moments of such tenderness that we all feel a lump in our throat. We can only hope that by some miracle Solo may survive until we return for another series: 'I reckon if Solo can make it among 12 large cubs he is going to be one tough customer to deal with when he grows up.'

Our audience were totally hooked by this story. People loved our animal characters: they invested in them emotionally and rooted for them when they were in trouble, celebrated their successes and grieved for their losses. Jeopardy – real-life, uncontrived jeopardy – was playing a powerful part in making the series a success.

**Opposite:** As the youngest member of the pride, Solo provided a constant source of fun and games for the older cubs. Because of the size difference he was forced to stand up for himself from an early age, developing into a powerful young male with attitude.
**Above:** Elephants must feed for up to 18 hours a day, with bulls eating up to 300 kg (660 lb) of vegetation to sustain their huge bulk.

# Swift and
# Enduring

The 2002 series – our fourth – would prove to be a watershed. By now we knew what worked and what didn't. We were beginning to see what made a good story – where the jeopardy lay to keep people watching. This is not as contrived as it might sound. Jeopardy envelops the lives of our big cats 24 hours a day; we just record it and have always prided ourselves on keeping *Big Cat* as real as possible.

On the technical side, having a DV director operating a hand-held digital video camera in the vehicle with each presenter every moment of the day provided an immediacy that was lacking in earlier programmes. This change in style meant the audience had a greater sense of

travelling with the presenters – you're in the car with us. The Natural History Unit had realised that there was room for a more 'popular' approach to natural-history film-making, and *Big Cat* was proving to be an important part of that. We had to stay current or we wouldn't survive. Natural history had a well-established and dedicated niche audience, but with a plethora of analogue and digital channels for people to choose from we wanted to tap into a wider public, drawing in those who loved animals but didn't necessarily want to know the details of their physiology. This was not as easy as it sounds: we needed to be entertaining without dumbing down.

Each time *Big Cat* was recommissioned we were expected to deliver the series on a reduced budget, and that meant fewer days in the field. It also meant plenty of pre-planning at every level. For one thing, tonnes of equipment had to be flown in from England and set up ahead of time. Governor's Camp was pivotal to this, outfitting a private camp for us and making sure that none of us got trampled by a hippo or flattened by a buffalo in the process. Governor's is actually the name of a 'family' of tented camps, another of which, known as Little Governor's – in a beautiful location on the other side of the river – would also play a key role in fulfilling our filming needs.

# bigCat diary

## A new *presenter*

The heart of the *Big Cat* crew remained remarkably consistent, but there were always some new faces to welcome. The biggest change in personnel was scripted by our executive producer, Fiona Pitcher. Fiona had made a name for herself finding new talent, and she produced a masterstroke by introducing a female presenter.

Saba Douglas-Hamilton was born in Kenya and has a Masters degree in anthropology. Her father, Iain, is a renowned conservationist who pioneered the first behavioural research of African elephants in the wild, and with his wife Oria campaigned successfully for many years to ban the ivory trade. Saba's intuitive understanding of wildlife comes from having been brought up in the bush amongst elephants, and trained at the knee by her zoologist parents. Saba brought a more instinctive approach to *Big Cat*; she wasn't afraid to express her feelings and the audience took an instant shine to her. She was to cut her teeth on the lions' story.

At the heart of the series, though, were still our big cats. With three to choose from, the moment the energy began to fade with any of our stories – cut. We kept reminding ourselves how lucky we were, but the truth is that the Mara is simply the finest area in the world for filming wildlife – not just big cats.

To maximise our filming opportunities, either Simon or I would head for the Mara before the main crew arrived to spend a few days with our producers and plan our stories: which of our star cats were still alive and making headlines, who had cubs and 'how were the Marsh Pride doing'. They were always our lions of choice, the easiest to find and, much to our delight, in 2002 they had young cubs for us to follow. Simon's cheetahs were not quite so straightforward. Amber had disappeared and none of the other females in the vicinity had cubs. However the Mara Triangle looked more promising: cheetahs do well here, perhaps because there are fewer lions and hyenas to trouble them. The balloon pilots who fly out of Little Governor's Camp each morning kept a careful eye on the area for us and reported back anything of interest – such as, we hoped, a cheetah family.

Elephant calves playing: milk tusks are shed in their second year

Black-backed jackal pups at their den

Olive baboons are born with a black coat and pixie-shaped ears

Female olive baboon: baboons are a major threat to leopards

In the end, what made the dry season of 2002 so memorable was that all three of our big cats had cubs, and cubs are like gold to wildlife film-makers. They guarantee plenty of activity during the daytime – the adults are much more likely to do something when they have cubs to feed, cubs to socialise with and, in the case of lions and leopards, cubs to protect from males seeking to kill them, and from predators. Having a third presenter in place meant that Simon and Saba could each concentrate on a single story, leaving me to find out what had happened to Solo the lion cub, and to try to catch up with Zawadi.

At the start of Programme 1, we meet Simon as he comes out of camp headed for the Triangle. 'We've already heard that there is a mother cheetah with four cubs.' It's still dark and the cheetah crew has quite a journey to make before they can start work.

Filming in the Triangle meant crossing the river at Mara Bridge – almost an hour's drive, with possibly another hour before reaching the cheetahs. That wouldn't do. So Simon and the cheetah crew left their vehicles parked at Little Governor's. All they had to do then was jump in the boat that ferries people back and forth on a rope. They would be up

Main picture: Members of the Marsh Pride resting on a termite mound in Musiara Marsh, the core of their dry-season territory.

at 5 am, grab their picnics, hitch a lift in a vehicle headed for the river, jump in the ferry, leg it through Little – avoiding any elephants and buffaloes on the way – then race the hot-air balloons across the plains to join their cheetah family. That was only possible because Japhet Kivango and the other spotters were already out on the plains locating our stars.

Kike, who became the star of the next series, sprinting flat out after a Thomson's gazelle – which she caught after a long chase. At top speed a cheetah can reach up to 112 km/h (70 mph).

**A constant search for food**
Honey and her cubs in the Mara Triangle. Cheetahs seem to thrive on these open plains with their scattered balanites trees. Honey often roamed back and forth across the Mara River in search of prey.

Knowing how difficult it is for a mother cheetah to raise cubs, Simon wasn't surprised to learn that there were now three rather than four. But even so he was happy to have a cat with cubs to follow in such a beautiful part of the Mara: 'It's always a delight to start watching a new family of cats, and cheetahs are without a doubt my favourites: Ferraris of the animal world, full of feline grace, built on a greyhound chassis. And the cubs have to be contenders for the cutest animals in Africa.'

Simon named the cheetah mother Honey – as he had named Amber – for the colour of her eyes. This is no coincidence: a cheetah's eyes really grab your attention. They are very large, designed to help the predator spot its prey long before being spotted itself. And when it came to hunting, Honey would prove to be in a class of her own.

Simon was driven by specialist camera guide David Breed, with Pete McCowen operating the DV camera for the sync pieces. Joining us for the first time was Duncan Chard, who would be Simon's producer. The boys were up to every trick in the book, such as a very slick rotating shot around Simon poised behind camera; split-screen images so you can see both the prey and the cheetah in the build-up to the hunt; funky camera moves including time lapses, and much more besides – as I was to find out, we presenters were barely able to move without someone recording it. Simon had a new mega telephoto lens so he could zoom in on hunts, and quality back-up in Warren Samuels, who was operating a second long lens. Warren turned out to be a star in the making himself, producing some extraordinary footage in the years to come. The cheetah team were laying down the challenge to the other crews to up their game. Each night we would gather in the production tent to check the storyboard on which our producers posted key sequences, highlighting how our cats were performing. It was very competitive – everyone wanted their contribution to be memorable and engaging – but that was no bad thing: there was lot at stake for all of us.

As Saba picks up the Marsh Lions' story, we find that the two Blonde Males who invaded the territory over two years ago are now firmly established as pride males. When the larger of them stops to mark a bush, Saba captures the moment...

'He's leaving a scent message for other lions, rubbing his face against the bushes and spraying them with his urine.' As one of the lionesses moves forward to greet him, Saba continues: 'What's so lovely about lions when they're being social is the way they're so tactile with one another. When they are parted they come and greet — a special greeting — and rub their faces and their entire bodies along each other. It's so important for lions to show their confidence in lion society, to always show that you're strong and oozing confidence, because when you don't you can lose everything that is important to you.'

Above: Young lions love to play, mimicking the skills they will need later in life for hunting and fighting.

Meanwhile, my mind was focused on other lions. I wanted to find out what had happened to Solo. He had been barely four months old when we finished filming two years ago and I very much doubted if he would have survived the rainy season, when prey becomes far scarcer and competition for food is more intense. But against all expectations, we soon located a strapping two-year-old, with the beginnings of what promised to be a fine mane sprouting from his neck

and chest. He was the right age and in the right area. But there was only one way to be sure it was Solo.

Simon and I had been keeping our own big cat diaries over the years, so I was able to turn to the page where I had pasted in Solo's picture. My son David had also carefully drawn the cub's whisker-spot markings — these remain the same throughout life and are as individual as human fingerprints. The audience were able to witness our identification for themselves:

A five-month-old cub greeting the older of the two Blonde Males. Cubs are often cautious when approaching adult males, unsure of their reception, yet fascinated by the physical presence of these great creatures.

I sit with our editor Andy Chastney as he pulls up an image of Solo as a cub on a laptop so we can compare it with footage we have just shot of our young male. It is Solo. And not only has he survived, he is stirring up a storm with one of his older male relatives.

The driver-guides at Governor's Camp keep a log of events in the area, enabling us to piece together the story. The two old pride males whom Angie and I had first seen in the Triangle in 1996 and who had lorded it over the Ridge Pride for more than four years had been ousted by younger, fitter nomadic males, who were now consorting with the lionesses from the Ridge Pride to the east of Paradise Plain. The break-up of the pride had forced Solo and the other subadults to flee. Now they roamed the no-man's land between Paradise Plain, Rhino Ridge and a strip of riverine forest bordering the Marsh Pride territory to the south of Governor's Camp. At some point Solo and one of the older subadults had broken away, intent on carving out a future together. If they survived the next two years they would be a force to be reckoned with – that much was already evident. This is a pattern that you see repeated time and again among lion prides: old males are replaced by younger ones, cubs are killed and subadults ousted. In time a new generation of cubs emerges, sired by the new pride males, and the process begins all over again.

*Fire sweeping through the Mara during the dry season*

As well as finding Solo alive and watching him more than hold his own in the company of his larger male companion, I have another cause for celebration: 'Can you believe it, no sooner have we arrived in the Mara than we get word that there's a leopard, possibly with cubs, right here in Leopard Gorge? It's got to be a leopard we know.' That means Zawadi. The last time I saw her, she was posing as good as gold on a termite mound along the flank of Leopard Gorge. That was in September 2001, shortly after she had lost her previous litter. A driver and his guests from Kichwa Tembo Camp had actually witnessed the birth of those cubs, proving what an exceptionally tolerant cat Zawadi is. Now, as we look for what I hope will be a new generation of her cubs, I explain that the gorge is in many ways the perfect place for a leopard to give birth: 'From up here she's got a perfect view of the surrounding countryside. She can see if there's danger approaching, if there are lions – and of course there are plenty of hyenas in this area – and she can check for prey.'

You can hear a waver in my voice as I speak these words. I am just so excited: years of hopes and expectations have gone into this moment. A leopard with young cubs in a place as beautiful as Leopard Gorge is a photographer's dream and what every visitor on safari would love to see. In fact, during filming I was approached by a family of visitors from America who some years earlier had bought a copy of a CD-Rom called *Safari* which Angie and I had produced and which featured a map with Leopard Gorge marked on it. They had hired a vehicle and driven to the gorge hoping to see a leopard. You can imagine their surprise when they found both me and a leopard with cubs in residence. If only it was always that easy!

My enthusiasm is soon shattered. As has happened so often in the past, Zawadi runs into trouble. Three weeks before filming began she produced three cubs in a fortress of a cave at the mouth of the gorge. A leopard often moves her cubs when they are small, probably to help prevent a build-up of scent. But Zawadi's latest hiding place, further down the gorge, is painfully inadequate. Not only is this cave easy to enter, but the hyenas soon come sniffing, attracted by the scent of a Thomson's gazelle that she has killed and hung in a tree right opposite: as we head home that night, we pass hyenas moving up the track in the direction of the kill.

By the following morning there is no sign of the gazelle and from Zawadi's nervous demeanour we can tell that something terrible has happened. The hyenas must have found the cubs – though not all of them. Zawadi has managed to carry one to safety further along the gorge and we capture some poignant moments of mother and cub together. Zawadi later moves the survivor 10 km (6 miles) to an area to the north known as Moses Rock, where she raised her daughter Safi. A few days later a grass fire sweeps through the area, but fortunately stops short of the cub's hiding place. In the end, however, it fails to survive and, in time-honoured leopard fashion, Zawadi disappears for a while – without cubs she is free to wander the full extent of her territory, making her much more difficult for us to locate.

Young cubs are adventurous and full of mischief; they love to scramble up into bushes and gnaw on twigs and branches.

Saba's assignment is proving to be more upbeat; she relishes the opportunity of watching the Marsh Pride with cubs: 'This is so exciting for me, the chance to follow one pride of lions for the next two months and spend every day in their company, getting to know them intimately.' But here too there is soon cause for concern...

**A balanced diet**
Kali with cubs aged about six months. Lions' adult teeth emerge at around 13-15 months, making it easier for them to hunt and to compete at kills.

Three of the Marsh Lionesses have recently given birth along the Bila Shaka Lugga. Two of them, Mama Lugga and White Eye – first-time mothers at four years of age – have three and four cubs respectively, all about four weeks old. Trouble is brewing for Mama Lugga as Saba sets the scene: 'They are utterly dependent on their mother for milk and protection. Their mother is the only contact they have with other lions at this early age and that allows a very strong bond to develop between a lioness and her cubs.' But Mama Lugga hasn't reckoned with the disruption that is about to be caused by some of her relatives – two larger female cubs of around seven and ten months. She does her best to dissuade the older cubs from playing with her babies, who can barely walk; she snarls and lunges, slapping the intruders aside. The two females mean no harm, but this is the last thing a mother wants – especially a new mother: 'It's vital now for her to reconnect with her cubs. She has to be the centre of their world.' This process of imprinting is vital if a mother is to raise her young successfully.

Left: White Eye with her ten-week-old cubs gambolling on a termite mound.
Above: After mating, a lioness turns on the male with an explosive snarl, telling him to back off.
Opposite: The Marsh Lionesses on the move, Mama Lugga leading the way and White Eye bringing up the rear. This pride usually numbers five or six lionesses accompanied by two or occasionally three pride males.

Sadly, in this instance, the damage has been done. While Mama Lugga is away hunting, White Eye and her own family come across the cubs, who – being of a similar age to White Eye's litter – follow White Eye when she departs again. When Mama Lugga returns to find her cubs gone, she wanders up and down the lugga, calling and sniffing for signs of their whereabouts. Saba picks up her story: 'Last time I saw this lioness she was very distressed. She's a first-time mother and her inexperience is really showing after losing her cubs to another female.

It is as if she's completely lost her maternal instincts.' To all intents and purposes it is as if Mama Lugga's cubs had died. The next thing we know, she is 3 km (2 miles) away in the marsh, mating with one of the Blonde Males, the father of her cubs.

Saba points up the irony: 'Whilst one mother has more cubs than she can cope with (lions only have four teats), the other has none.' Fortunately lionesses in a pride – all of whom are related – co-operate in raising their cubs. They do this most efficiently when similar-aged cubs come together

to form a crèche. As chance would have it, Kali – White Eye's and Mama Lugga's aunt – has brought her three cubs to join the other two litters, making a total of ten youngsters. Mama Lugga's cubs are in good hands: 'This crèche was formed just in time to act as a safety net. The sisterhood has worked. These two related females will look after all the cubs. Even at this young age the cubs develop ties that will last them a lifetime and are the very foundation of lion society. The more companions you have the stronger you are.' The crèche system

helps to promote the development of large groups of same-sex relatives, enabling them to start life with the best chance of acquiring a territory. In addition, White Eye and Kali are very tough customers who will not put up with any nonsense from the two young females who caused Mama Lugga such problems, or their side-kick Kijana, an 18-month-old male. These three young lions are inseparable and tag along with an adult lioness called Nusu Nusu. We will see more of Kijana and Nusu Nusu in years to come.

# bigCat diary

## Lion fact file...

### I recognise you!
A lion's whisker spots are unique and remain the same all its life, enabling us to identify individuals. This is Kali.

### Night vision
A layer of reflective cells in a cat's retina (called the tapetum) makes its nocturnal vision six times as powerful as ours.

### A 'flehmen' face
This strange grimace shows that the lion has picked up an interesting scent – possibly a female in season.

# Close encounters

One morning, rubbing the sleep from our eyes, we hear Saba calling on her car radio. She is still in camp and so are two of the Marsh Lions – Split Nose and Lispy, also known as the Blonde Sisters: 'Just goes to show, you can look for these lions all day long, then they pitch up in your camp first thing in the morning.'

I had had a similar experience some 20 years earlier, but on foot.

*'Binoculars at the ready' is one of the first rules of big cat watching*

The *Big Cat* Camp is situated on a beautiful bend in the river, a popular location for visitors to step out of their car to look at the pod of hippos slumbering on a comfortable sand bank below. In the dry season it is also a wonderful place to watch elephants drinking and crossing the river. It was with these thoughts in mind that I drove up the narrow track leading through the dense patch of forest shrouding the water's edge. I stepped out of my vehicle and continued on foot, keeping a close watch for hippos or buffaloes. I had paused at the base of the same giant greenheart tree more times than I can remember, always checking in case there was anything lying there. And on this occasion there was – a huge male lion, sitting up alert, looking me straight in the eye. Before I could blink he turned and bounded away – I can still hear the sound of his feet thumping the ground, the sharp intake of breath as he grunted out a warning as I stood riveted to the spot. All I could think was, 'Imagine if that had been a buffalo.'

If that wasn't exciting enough, things don't come any scarier than when Honey and her cubs come face to face with a full-grown male lion over in the Triangle. She flatterns herself against the ground, nervously looking back over her shoulder for her cubs. They are confused and terrified; one tries to crawl away: 'Oh my God, don't let this happen,' implores Simon. The look on the lion's face says it all. He sees a rival and wants to kill it. The cubs wait for Honey's next move. She arches her back and lowers her head, adopting a hunched, crab-like posture that makes her look bigger, drawing the lion to her. She runs, then stops, encouraging him to chase her, leading him away from her cubs, then stops again: 'Honey, remarkable and brave cat that she is, is holding her ground. Let it be over, let it be over.'

This kind of behaviour looks suicidal, but generally it is a very effective way for a cheetah mother to protect her cubs – what else can she do? Cheetahs are so much smaller and weaker than lions that they cannot afford to fight; even when they run it can occasionally prove fatal, as may have been the case with Amber's mother, who was either ambushed by lions or a leopard or killed trying to defend her five young cubs.

In the end the lion loses interest – he can't catch Honey, and her cubs have kept their cool. As she walks back to them they jump up against her, embracing her in their paws, licking her face. Simon breathes a sigh of relief: 'That is what I call a joyful reunion.'

By now the sun has set; it will be dark in half an hour. Time to head for camp with a sense of deep satisfaction; a quick shower from a bucket of hot water suspended above the tent, followed by a drink and a chat around the camp fire will soon help revive weary bodies. Then, depending on how drained you feel, a plate of food or just a bowl of soup before crawling dog-tired into bed.

For me, the most memorable scene of 2002 came towards the end of the series. We had already managed to catch up with three-year-old Safi and the huge male leopard who had established himself as the territory-holder. But now, in our final week of filming, we really wanted to track down Zawadi, and what better place to search than Leopard Gorge?

It is early in the morning and I can hear the telltale sound of hyraxes calling. I stop the vehicle. Then, as is often the way with leopards, I realise that Zawadi is there, sitting right in front of me further down the track – it is only when she moves her head

that I can distinguish her outline against the camouflage of rocks and dense vegetation. I catch my breath, speechless with emotion and excitement – you can hear it in the pause of recognition, the momentary stunned silence: 'Oh my, right in front of me, what a stroke of luck. She's going to come right towards our car. She doesn't give us a second glance. It's as if we weren't here and that's the way I like it.' Zawadi hesitates, sniffs the vegetation, reading the scent, then continues on her way up the gorge. 'Now wasn't that a little moment of magic? I can't believe she did that.'

I don't mean I am surprised by her actions – only that I can hardly believe our luck that Zawadi has performed such a perfect endpiece to close out our leopard viewing.

In fact Zawadi has another finale to share with us, a dramatic curtain call. We find her hunting along a lugga close to the gorge. Her target is a wart hog with a family of piglets, a perfect snack if she can outwit the mother. Sure enough, she launches her attack and snatches up one of the piglets. But just as certainly, the mother pig tears after her as she races for the safety of a nearby tree. Zawadi reaches

the tree just as the wart hog delivers a glancing blow to her spotted flank, hooking at her with razor-sharp tusks. I expect to see a gaping wound, blood at least. But showing all her athleticism and phenomenal strength Zawadi manages to cling to the tree – stretched out at 90 degrees to the trunk, held there by a single front paw as she flies through the air. Then she bounds higher, the piglet still kicking as its mother races away in pursuit of her surviving young.

If the leopards are buzzing, the lions are roaring – literally. The larger of the two Blonde Males provides Saba with a Pavarotti moment that leaves her speechless. As Saba sits and watches, the old male suddenly starts to roar. At first he lies there, every muscle in his massive body straining with the effort. Then he stands, 1.5 m (5 ft) from the front of Saba's car, roaring his head off. In a magnificent show of cool he stretches – one of those 'only a cat can do' stretches that feels good just to watch. Saba later describes this as 'one of the most meaningful and awesome moments. I just had tears in my eyes. I was absolutely convinced that he had come to say goodbye because he knew we were leaving. What a fantastic end to *Big Cat Diary*.'

**Opposite:** Some male cheetahs never manage to hold a territory and are known as 'floaters'. Such males – most commonly singletons – need to be constantly on the move to avoid competition with residents. The stress of this lifestyle is probably the reason they suffer poorer health and become susceptible to diseases such as mange.
**Above:** Zawadi poised to hunt. The best chance of seeing a leopard on the move is to be up before dawn or at dusk.

The *Big Cat Week* logo appears briefly on the screen, fading. Cut to cheetah racing through the long grass as I exclaim: 'Look at that, she's going, she's going, look at her go – she's got the baby, she's got the baby topi, and the mother's coming straight back, she's coming straight back.' The topi calf bleats in distress, a sound guaranteed to whip its mother's maternal instincts into a frenzy.

The cheetah picks the calf up and takes a few bounding steps towards the topi mother, who is not intimidated in the least. 'She's moving in to attack, there she goes, and the cheetah's coming right at us. Here she comes, here she comes, here she comes, right on the car. Boy oh boy, did you hear the noise of the mother, did you see the look on Kike's face?' By now the audience are not only riveted by the pace

of the action and the fact that they have just watched a cheetah leap onto my car for refuge, but they are probably chuckling at the look of wide-eyed astonishment on my face. It is one of those once-in-a-lifetime moments when the power of nature is captured in all its raw intensity. What an introduction to *Big Cat Week* and Kike the cheetah.

# Mother
# Courage

# big**Cat** diary

# A change of Format

7:88:39PM

Over the years *Big Cat* had moved closer and closer to our initial concept – a genuine reality programme filmed in the moment. It had also spawned a whole genre of siblings – *Elephant Diaries, Big Bear Diary, Orang Utan Diary* and *Chimpanzee Diary*, all of which relied on a similar formula of strong, intimate stories focusing on the individual characters of our animal stars. The powers that be now felt that we were 'entertaining' enough for BBC1 and, as part of the transition, took the decision to present the show in a different format. Instead of it being broadcast once a week for a run of six to eight weeks, it was to be stripped across a single week in a prime-time slot at 7 pm, 30 minutes before the soaps.

*Big Cat Week* proved an instant success, doubling our audience from a very respectable 3 million viewers on BBC2 to 6 million on BBC1. It peaked at 7 million, making it one of the most popular shows on television that week.

People loved the sense of an event, of sitting down at the same time each evening and tapping into the highs and lows of the cats' daily lives. Although it was filmed over the course of a month, it had the feel of live television, the safari experience brought right into your living room.

*Big Cat* is mostly edited in a production tent in the bush, with only 'tweaking' done back at the NHU in Bristol. This was the Edit Suite set up in camp for *Big Cat Live*. Narration is kept to a minimum – 90 per cent of what the audience hear us say is filmed 'in the moment'.

Angie combines game-spotting with taking the production stills for *Big Cat*. A cheetah like Kike is a dream for any photographer.

Angie and I knew Kike intimately, but while I had kept close tabs on the Marsh Lions over the years and always thought of the leopard as my favourite big cat, I never invested the same amount of time with cheetahs. That changed when Angie and I were asked to write books on each of our three big cats as tie-ins to the TV series. When the time came to work on the cheetah book I asked if I could move to presenting the cheetahs' story, relinquishing the leopards to Saba – and what a stroke of luck that proved to be for me. Kike was special.

We had seen mother topis confront cheetahs before – their belligerent roar of defiance is often enough to spook a predator – and Kike had taken her habit of jumping on to vehicles to new levels of audacity. But capturing such a moment on film is an entirely different matter. Our wildlife cameraman Warren Samuels and his driver Wilson Wemali were ace at covering high-action sequences, and DV cameraman Toby Strong had an artistic and intuitive feel for wildlife and people, instantly panning onto Kike as she tore towards the car before cutting back to me for my startled reaction.

As luck would have it, soundman Andy Hawley was with me that day – he rotated between the three big cat crews, spending a few days with each before moving on. Andy's presence ensured that everything from the mother topi's cries to the sound of Kike's feet pounding across my bonnet, interspersed with my excited narration, were crystal clear; this would help grab the audience's attention and keep them watching throughout the week. In fact this sequence was to earn the cheetah team a place in the top three most memorable factual moments on television that year.

## Introducing Kike

It's time to introduce Kike properly to our audience. She leaps onto the bonnet of my car, relaxed and elegant, exuding confidence and athleticism, while her three nine-month-old cubs race around the vehicle in a frenzy of excitement: 'OK, there is only one wild cheetah that does that and it's Kike. Is she a wild cheetah? You better believe it. This is a cheetah who hunts, who does everything you'd expect a cheetah in the Mara to do. The only difference is she uses these cars to her advantage; they've been part of her life for six years, ever since she was a tiny cub...'

Meanwhile the cubs have scrambled up onto the two spare wheels on the back of my vehicle, as bold as brass, relying on the rough tread of the tyres for balance – at this young age this is easier for them than trying to jump on the slick surface of the bonnet.

Kike is thought to be one of Amber's offspring and with three hungry mouths to feed she's always on the look-out for prey. Sometimes she launches herself off the car straight into a hunt, leaving Toby and me scrambling to cover the action, just when we thought it was safe to eat. Food and plastic containers fly around the car, scattering mango chutney and beans all over our feet. Often the hunt ends in failure: 'Most of the time the predators don't catch what they are trying to hunt. The prey animals have all kinds of tricks to avoid being eaten', such as when a gazelle fawn lies chin to the ground in a posture of concealment or a wart hog piglet suddenly dives into a burrow.

It's Saba's turn to show what she's made of when her vehicle gets stuck trying to cross a gully along the Talek River while she is searching for leopards. She rises to the challenge and soon hoists the high-lift jack into place, then drives off in a cloud of dust. Zawadi is proving hard to find, so Saba decides to follow up a tip-off about another female: 'It's all right for the boys, they've got a huge pride of lions and four beautiful cheetahs right out in the open. But searching for a leopard is like chasing shadows.' Nonetheless, with the help of our spotters, Saba soon discovers that the leopard in question has two three-month-old cubs. Saba names the mother

Above: Bella and cub along the Talek River – the perfect setting for our leopard family.
Opposite: Kike lying on the roof of my vehicle. Cheetah photography will never be easier than this.

Bella and watches in excited fascination as the cubs gambol alongside her, biting at her legs and hanging on to her flanks: 'Every single little thing they do, every pounce, every sprint, every bite of the neck is something that's going to help them later on in life and hone their hunting techniques.' The gods were certainly smiling on us in this first series of *Big Cat Week* – all three of our cats had cubs.

Simon certainly has reason to celebrate. The Marsh Lions are on top form. We see him watching as a mob of lions streams past his vehicle, 29 in all in a single extended family: 'This is rush hour Masai Mara style. Everyone is filing home after a hard night's work, but of course the commuters here are lions.' Simba, the younger of the two Blonde Males, is in magnificent condition, though his older companion is missing, killed in an encounter with a buffalo some months earlier. Simon ponders Simba's future as a lone pride male: 'How long will his reign last?' Our spotters have already located two young nomads hanging around the periphery of the Marsh Pride territory. Trouble is brewing for Simba and his family.

Simon decides to focus his attention on a lioness known as Bibi – Kali's daughter – who at just under five years old is somewhat younger than Mama Lugga and White Eye. She is a relatively inexperienced mother with two cubs aged eight to ten weeks. Simon explains Bibi's dilemma: 'If just one [lioness in a pride] has a young family, then very often the other females in the group will shun the other. She is getting told off, beaten up and kicked out at the moment.'

While male lions fight over access to females, for the lionesses it is all about defending their territory against rival groups of females. Their wars are long-term affairs about real estate, a place to hunt and raise their young: there is only so much prime property to

go round. For the Marsh Pride, the Bila Shaka Lugga and the forest at the centre of the marsh are the very heart of their territory. Lions gravitate towards core areas such as these when under threat, defending them tenaciously against outsiders. They may, however – albeit grudgingly at times – allow their grown offspring to camp on the periphery of their territory: it is better to share with relatives than with strangers. In fact large prides seek to extend their sphere of influence when they can, bullying neighbouring prides into ceding some of their land: land that may ultimately help younger female relatives such as Bibi to survive.

If Bibi is struggling, then so too is the father of her cubs. The two nomadic males have moved in,

determined to oust Simba. Overthrow attempts often happen when lions are at their most active, shrouded by darkness. The following morning the only signs that anything has happened may be pawfuls of mane, perhaps a trail of blood – and at times a dead lion. But not all pride takeovers end in violence. Sometimes the old territory-holders simply turn their backs and run; they may even manage to regroup and in time take control of another pride.

This time, however, the action takes place by daylight. Simon catches up with the two young males one morning as they pursue Simba through acres of long golden grass: 'It's happening right before our eyes. My worst fears are coming true. Simba is in deep trouble.' Simon's face is tense, his voice urgent, his excitement in filming something unusual tempered by his concern for lions he knows intimately: 'This is going to be a fight for sure.'

Above: One of the three males who ousted Notch (see Chapter 9). All cats advertise their presence by marking 'scent posts' in their territory with their individually identifiable scent.
Opposite: Roaring is another way that both lions and leopards (but not cheetahs) communicate their presence – a lion can be heard at least 5 km (3 miles) and possibly 8 km (5 miles) away.

# bigcat diary

## Seconds count

At key moments in the action it is critical that everyone stays calm; get it wrong and you either miss the shot or disturb the animals and the moment fades. As the nomads approached Simba, Dave Breed was keen to move the camera vehicle to get a better angle for Simon – it was risky but if it paid off everyone would be more than happy. Simon was trying to film and commentate at the same time, no easy matter when you need to keep your eye to the viewfinder, gather your thoughts and sound coherent. But Dave had to break in. Simon agreed: 'Interrupt me whenever.' Dave moved hurriedly – it was his call, and the right one.

Things are not looking good for Simba, and Simon knows it: 'He looked so stable, so secure, definitely the king of his patch. And then it all looks so shaky so quickly when the competition moves in.' Simba continues on his way, eyes dead ahead, almost nonchalant; any sign of weakness or apprehension will spark an attack. The young males smell victory but are in no hurry. It's as if they know that their moment is coming – if not now, then very soon. One of them has a look of intense menace, head held low as if stalking prey, mouth tense. He means business. The other – younger, blonder, less sure of himself – is nevertheless ready to follow his companion's lead. Simba senses that he has no option but to flee, with Simon urging him on: 'Go, Simba, run, boy, run….' And run he does, with the two males

The Blonde Males strutting their stuff. The larger and older of them (on the left) was killed by a buffalo in May 2003, leaving his smaller companion Simba to fend for himself.

pursuing him across the plains. The tension is almost unbearable – but the audience will have to wait until tomorrow evening to learn what happens next.

Next morning there is no sign of Simba, prompting Simon to voice his concerns: 'Is he hiding, is he injured, is he dead?' We just don't know, but one thing is for certain – with both Simba and Bibi captivating our audience, Simon and the lion team are on a roll.

**Stars of Big Cat diary**

**Pride of place**
Simba being greeted by a lioness. Although a single lion rarely manages to claim a pride for himself, Simba (like Scar before him and Notch after) was able to cling on to his territory after his companion was killed.

**An excuse for a lie-in**
Kike and cubs on a chilly Mara morning. Cheetahs often remain tucked away until the sun has warmed them: this also reduces the chances of bumping into lions or hyenas that have been active during the night.

Like Bibi, Kike was also a single mother. Male cheetahs mate, then move on, covering as much ground as possible in their search for females; they play no part in rearing cubs. It was an extraordinary experience for me to spend time with Kike and her family, week after week, getting to know her routine, to feel something of her inner being. To have a cheetah sitting up on the roof of my car – within touching distance – knowing that as far as this gentle cat was concerned I was safe, allowed me to view cheetahs in a totally different way. But we were all very aware of the responsibility that came with this privilege: 'It would be just so tempting to reach up and touch her, but it is an absolute no. You never do that, that would break the boundary. This is a wild cheetah. The only difference is that she treats every car as a mobile termite mound.' And mobile was right – some drivers took liberties with Kike; one even began to drive off when starting his engine proved insufficient to prompt her to clamber down. We were afraid that she might slip and injure a leg, and there were occasions when this almost happened.

Kike's cubs were full of nonsense, chasing around and under the car, leaping up to grab Andy Hawley's fluffy microphone or stalking a party of ground hornbills: giant black birds with distinctive red wattles and pickaxe bills that can tease a terrapin from its shell as easily as digging into rock-hard earth to uncover an insect larva. The cubs were learning 'what is prey and what isn't, what can you eat and what can't you eat, and in this case what can fly and what can't'. They certainly knew what to do when their mother brought a gazelle fawn back to them, allowing them to practise their hunting skills, though there were times when the hyenas cut short their games. And by the end of the series they were prepared to chase topi calves with real intent – until the mother turned and sent them running back to Kike.

One of Kike's cubs in a tug-of-war with Andy Hawley's sound gear, to the amusement of DV director Toby Strong and myself. Kike lies in the shade, seemingly without a care in the world.

## Nothing doing!

Not every day was filled with action; far from it. All the teams faced long periods when nothing happened, as Simon explained: 'A big cat's life is one of short bursts of excitement followed by long hours of simply relaxing. The Big Cat team has to live on the same time-scale, which means hours and hours – and hours – of doing absolutely nothing.'

Spending time with a wild creature like
Kike was one of the highlights of my life.
She seemed totally oblivious to my presence.

Scent-marking and calling are vitally important ways for big cats to communicate with members of their own species. For the most part they try to avoid conflict by reading these messages and moving away from trouble, but sometimes they find themselves within view of a potential rival, as happened when Kike suddenly came face to face with another female cheetah, bent on trouble. We see Kike hold her position crouched on a termite mound while her cubs take refuge from the sun under Angie's vehicle, oblivious to the drama: 'It is apparent that the newcomer is young and pregnant, and she's intent on forcing Kike to move on: the area is swarming with Thomson's gazelles, many of whom have dropped their fawns since it started to rain: this makes it ideal hunting territory for cheetahs and the young female may be looking for a suitable place to have her cubs. Kike disappears behind the termite mound, then turns and yips submissively as the pregnant female bounds towards her, hackles raised in a menacing manner. The young female stops when she sees Kike's cubs moving out from under Angie's vehicle. Four cheetahs are more than she has bargained for; she's made her point, and she turns and slinks away. In due course the young female gives birth though none of the cubs survive. I am almost certain that this is our first encounter with Shakira, whom we meet again in Chapter 7.

Meanwhile, the leopard crew found life even more taxing, driving for nearly an hour each morning and evening just to reach the Talek River where their quest would begin. There were times, though, when all the long hours of waiting paid off for Saba: 'Every now and then with Bella there are moments when her world just opens up that take my breath away.' We knew that having a mother leopard with cubs was the ultimate game-viewing experience – but would it last?

A large troop of olive baboons sweeping across the river towards the cubs made Saba anxious: 'After lions and hyenas, baboons are the most dangerous animals a leopard can encounter.' I had seen that for myself on many occasions when watching Half-Tail along Fig Tree Ridge and Leopard Gorge, where the baboons often roosted at night. If they spotted her, the baboons would chase her, even reach out to try to grab and bite her. Adult leopards have been mobbed and killed by baboons in circumstances such as these; cubs wouldn't stand a chance.

As is customary for a mother leopard, Bella often left her cubs on their own while she went off hunting. The two cubs were already aware of the dangers of crossing open spaces, clinging to cover and keeping their bodies close to the ground. Baboons, though, are crafty. With their keen eyes and well-developed colour vision there is not much that they do not see. If they spot danger, the big males invariably come and investigate, bristling with aggression and barking out far-ranging alarm calls to alert the rest of the troop. We see one male strut right up to a cave in the bank of the river, just above a fallen log where one of the cubs has sought sanctuary. He shakes the bush at the entrance to the crevice violently, snapping a branch in frustration and intimidation. But leopards are wily creatures too and the cubs have already learnt where to hide in these circumstances; the moment passes without further incident.

# big cat diary

## Toilet *humour!*

Amid the drama, there were fun moments, none more so than when Kike decided to use my vehicle as a latrine, just as she would a termite mound, squatting above my head and peeing or pooing through the open roof hatch. I never imagined that this would be my ultimate claim to fame, but I can always tell from the look of sheer pleasure on people's faces when they ask if I am the bloke from the telly that the cheetah crapped on! It was amusing to begin with, but believe me cheetah poo is very smelly and by the time Kike had pooped down the camera bags sewn into the front seat of my vehicle, peed in my eye – and much more besides – I was only too happy to close the hatch. The problem was the hatch needed to be open so that the sun could illuminate my face for the camera. And so it continued, much to everyone's delight.

*Kike's toilet antics gave us lots of laughs, but were indescribably smelly*

While jeopardy was, as ever, the order of the day, there were occasions when we simply relished the beauty and tranquillity of the Mara, when the light was almost unbearably beautiful with golden dawns or towering thunderheads. The arrival of the wildebeest and zebras added colour and drama to the landscape, reminding us of the power of nature to inspire humanity. Elephants paraded across the plains, at times forcing the mighty lions to give way.

These peaceful moments were balanced by times of real drama, such as when Simon witnessed the Marsh Pride at their most deadly. The plains were covered with wildebeest, zebras and topis, but a pride this size has the collective power to tackle even larger and more formidable prey – buffaloes. The incident starts with a single experienced lioness stalking through the long grass; 'every step a whisper' as Simon describes it. Too late the buffalo realises the danger, lifts its head, straining with nostrils flared as it picks up the scent of lion, the whites of its eyes bulging with fear as it sees the lioness. Its only chance is to charge forward, a brave but ultimately futile gesture of defiance. By now the rest of the pride have closed in, the two-and-a-half-year-old male Kijana adding his considerable bulk and power to the fray by leaping onto the buffalo's back, biting into its spine as it bucks and swings its massive horned head to try to shake off its

tormentors. The year-old cubs are 'learning their trade here and a difficult trade it is,' says Simon. The key moment is when one of the older, most experienced females – Kali or Notch, it's difficult to tell – grabs the cow by the nose to give it 'a kiss of death, to completely smother the mouth and nose of the buffalo with its own mouth'. Meanwhile the rest of the pride start to eat the buffalo alive – but we don't show that.

Angie and I have a soft spot for Bibi. We watched her in early 2000 when her mother Kali gave birth to a new litter. At one-and-a-half-years old, Bibi was a gentle lioness who loved to play with the cubs as much as they did with her; she was fascinated by her younger half-brothers and sisters and would spend hours in their company, fine-tuning her maternal instincts in the process.

Bibi isn't a complete outcast. Her cubs were sired by Simba, and Simon soon discovers that Bibi is 'shadowing the rest of the pride, never getting too close – 2 km or so [1¼ miles] – within sight and smell of the rest of the lions'. But she has to be careful now that the two nomadic males have moved in. On one occasion the lion crew films her standing her ground, fronting up to the males, threatening them with snarls and grunts, letting them know they are unwelcome. You can almost feel the loneliness of these single females; lions thrive in the company of their relatives and allies and seem somehow diminished in their absence.

By contrast, leopards are supremely adapted to a solitary existence, pound for pound the strongest and the wiliest of the three big cats. A leopard with cubs will often hunt during the daytime and over the years Bella has become a specialist in hunting wildebeest. For much of the year she feasts on Thomson's gazelles, supplemented by wart hog piglets, bushbuck, impalas, dik-dik, even Egyptian geese and white storks at times. But the migration provides a 'whole new world of opportunity for our predators', says Saba, and the scenes of massed herds of wildebeest swirling around the grasslands and sweeping down to the

Talek River are simply stunning this year. Bella's favourite technique is to ambush the animals when they come to drink or cross. She knows the crossing points intimately and uses the shielding presence of the riverbank as a blind, running as smooth as silk low to the ground across the open patches. Leopards are so quick and agile: 'Every muscle in her body is poised to strike.' A sudden short rush and Bella has a wildebeest calf by the throat, pinning it to the ground. She lies there in the open, shielding herself from the stampeding herd behind the body of her victim, then releases it to grab another calf, felling it with a flying tackle of such power and violence that it is slammed to the ground before it knows what has hit it.

Saba explains Bella's feast-or-famine strategy: 'That is more than any leopard can eat in a sensible amount of time, but she is just going to stock up while she has the chance.' Sometimes in circumstances such as this you see a leopard resting contentedly in a tree surrounded by two or three carcasses that it will consume at its leisure. But not in this instance. Shaken and somewhat wobbly, the first calf recovers and totters off back to the herd as Bella drags her latest victim to cover.

Bibi gave birth at a time when none of the other lionesses in the pride had young cubs and for a while was forced to live the life of an outsider. However she was eventually accepted back into the pride and her cubs survived.

101

While Bella is providing plenty of food for her cubs, Bibi's two youngsters are receiving a somewhat brutal introduction to family life in the Marsh Pride. It is one of the most harrowing episodes in the series. Bibi is nowhere to be seen. Perhaps she has gone off hunting, which may be just as well. Before they know what is happening the two little cubs, who until now have had contact only with their mother, are being mobbed by a dozen or more youngsters from the pride. Pushed, pawed and prodded, they squawk and grizzle with fear and apprehension, their teeth bared, ears flattened against their heads. Simon can hardly watch: 'I don't think I can bear the tension of this. If it was just a handful of cubs we could begin to relax, but every member of the pride wants to inspect them.' For a moment the situation looks as if it might turn ugly, with the cubs killed or injured, but eventually the pride move off, leaving the cubs shaken but unharmed.

In the course of the next few days Simon manages to track Bibi down and is overjoyed when the two cubs emerge from a hollow at the base of an enormous strangler fig known as Dave's Tree, a landmark in the centre of the marsh where the crews sometimes gather for a sundowner.

Before the end of the series Saba has enjoyed some wonderfully intimate moments with Bella and her cubs, watching as they suckle and groom, struggle up the steep face of the river bank, stalk wading birds or chase butterflies. 'What I really like about Bella is that she has a slightly grizzled edge to her. She's a beautiful cat, but she's old – about seven years or so – her experience and the wear and tear of the years really show. Her ability to raise her cubs successfully to adulthood is going to rely very much on what she's learned throughout all of her years.' At that the leopard gently picks up one of the cubs in her mouth and carries it out of the tree. We will see much more of Bella in the years to come.

Simon has been fortunate to watch over the Marsh Pride at the height of its powers. Near the end of filming he finds the pride feasting on a kill,

their hoary breath crystallising in the cold morning air. It is a primeval scene, raw and unforgiving, such is the strident theatre of lion politics: 'The thunderous voices are not Simba, not even the adult females, but the cubs.' Each is determined to fight for its share of the spoils to the extent that one youngster lashes out at Simba, slapping at his face, not in the least bit intimidated when the pride male retaliates, albeit pulling his punches. With weapons designed to slash and maim, even the youngest lion deserves and at times receives respect – they are as hard as nails. Simba's tolerance is born of self-interest – he has invested in the cubs' future – but as Simon says, at some point 'Simba will have to stand and fight or run

for his life again.' In fact Simba does have support of sorts. Kijana, who was a gangly one-and-a-half-year-old when we last filmed him, is now three years old and still tolerated by the females in the pride and by the old pride male. Perhaps together they can fend the nomads off for a while longer.

For my part I can't help but marvel once again at this extraordinary land which Angie and I are so fortunate to call our second home: 'It's such a magical place: the landscape, the colours, the sunsets, but best of all our incredible big cats, the lions, leopards and of course the cheetahs. The Mara always delivers for us – hope to see you next year.'

Becoming
Independ

Once again *Big Cat Week* opens with a bang: no frills, straight into our story. I'm standing in the camera door of my vehicle, slightly manic, watching as Kike's three adolescent offspring – two females and a male – launch themselves from their resting place among a clump of bush out into the blistering midday heat. 'Go, go, go,' I urge. Their quarry is a party of four male Thomson's gazelles who have unwittingly grazed closer and closer to the watching predators. The youngsters are hungry, ready to put everything into the chase. It is the two females who lead the charge up the hill as the Tommies race away, but there is no escape as they zigzag across the landscape. I need to move closer: 'Chuck out the tea – to hell with that – wow, that is about the longest cheetah chase I have ever seen – that was ballistic.'

Watching this piece of footage now, I ponder on its appropriateness: I know Angie thought I went over the top. If I was on my own or with her photographing the cats, I wouldn't utter a word, but at the time my response felt totally natural. Completely caught up in the moment, I really wanted the young cheetahs to succeed – my loyalties were to them and them alone. The sequence certainly has energy and the editors loved it, but I'm still not sure.

Me at my happiest – out in the bush watching wild animals

## The audience approves...

The first series of *Big Cat Week* had gone down a storm. The audience approval ratings went through the roof; everyone was talking about the show and wanted more. Stripping the series across a single week had really worked and it seemed an obvious decision to do it again...

*Zebras are an important prey species for lions*

By the time we started filming in August 2004 the migration was in full flood. The light was stunning and so was the number of animals. In a good year the Mara plays host to over half a million wildebeest and around 100,000 zebras: the land reverberates to their voices. When they depart, the area looks strangely empty, even though there are tens of thousands of resident animals whose wanderings are of a lesser order – the buffaloes, giraffes, topis, Coke's hartebeests, wart hogs and impalas, to mention just a few – and for the territorial lions at least it is these resident prey populations that determine their numbers. But the great herds would be with us for a while yet and for as long as they were the predators could feast.

Early on in the series I caught up with my old friend Kike. She was up to her familiar tricks, peeing on the windscreen, pooping on the roof hatch, even on me at times. But she had yet to produce another litter of cubs and we knew from past experience that the story of a single cheetah was probably too one-paced to hold our audience's interest. We were desperate to catch up with Kike's newly independent

**Stars of big Cat diary**

**No time to relax**
Stashing a kill in a tree doesn't always protect a leopard from eagles and vultures! After carrying her meal back to ground level, Half-Tail (when she still had her tail) dragged it to a croton thicket and fed in peace.

One of the Ridge Pride cubs on a zebra kill.
A pride of lions is generally powerful enough
to be able to feed undisturbed: for hyenas
to win possession of a carcass generally
takes four of them to every lioness.

youngsters, whom Angie and I had last seen with
their mum in April. But sibling groups such as these
travel widely in their search for food, often moving
at night, and I doubted that we would be able to
keep up with them even if we found them. We did
have a second option, however – or so we thought.
Much to everyone's delight Honey and her latest
litter of three-quarter-grown cubs had left the
Triangle a few months earlier and had been roaming
around Paradise Plain and the Musiara area ever
since. They were exactly what we were looking for,
but just as we thought our problems were solved they
crossed the Talek River and disappeared into the
acacia woodlands to the south.

On the other hand, Saba and the leopard team
were in high spirits. The previous year it had often
taken all day to find Bella – if they found her at all
– despite the fact that she had young cubs. But this
time luck was with us and on the first day in the
field they found Chui, Bella's 15-month-old-son,
who was proving to be a bit of a star himself.
Saba explained how she could distinguish Chui
from other leopards in the area. Each individual
has a unique pattern of spots and in Chui's case
four distinctive spots at the centre of the spotted
necklace around his neck were a giveaway. Chui
was 'still very much dependent on Bella for most of
his food', tracking her down by scent and the sound
of her distinctive rasping contact call. His sister had
disappeared six months earlier, probably killed by
the leopard's greatest enemy after man – lions.

# Spotting a Leopard

One of the key people on the leopard team is photographer Ian Johnson. Ian learned his bush craft and tracking skills in South Africa and for him the Talek area is a joy: it has one of the highest concentrations of leopards he has ever experienced – there is just so much prey for them.

Early each morning Ian and the spotters spread out across Bella's territory like detectives collecting evidence on a missing person, scouring the thickets and trees for clues. There are a number of hot spots which attract prey, particularly during the dry season when they need to drink. The raucous noise of animals gathering at these places is guaranteed to attract an ambush specialist such as Bella. Like all our big cats, Bella favours vehicle tracks – they act as convenient marking points and scent trails and provide good visibility and easy walking. When the grass is long she can stalk along these pathways unseen.

When tracking leopards, Ian tries to think like one, doing everything he can to get inside his quarry's head, guided by his hunches as to her current location and what she might do next. He will spend hours scanning with his binoculars, covering the same ground again and again if necessary, looking and listening for anything that might give him a clue to her whereabouts: scats, tracks, alarm calls – particularly guinea fowls, jackals, hyrax, even cisticolas (tiny warbler-like birds that alarm-call in the presence of leopards). Finding a leopard is never going to be easy, but Ian's skills certainly improve our chances.

Saba tracks Bella
along the Jalek River

If Ian Johnson is a bonus to the leopard team (see box), then Warren Samuels and his driver Wilson Wemali provide a similar service to the cheetah crew. With the help of our other spotters, Chris Brennan, Samuel Ruto and Jacob Lelesara, we eventually managed to locate the young cheetahs, and it wasn't long before they were in trouble. One of the young females managed to hook herself through the nose on a branch in thick bush. The more she tried to pull free the deeper and more tenaciously the thorns dug into her nostril. This kind of thorn bush is known as 'wait-a-bit' for this very reason – you think you can pull free but you can't. It looked excruciatingly painful and the female's distress soon attracted the attention of her brother, who proceeded to paw and slap at the branch before licking the blood from his sister's face – they had evidently fed earlier in the day, a good sign. Fortunately the branch eventually jerked free.

**Above:** Cheetahs, the most specialist of the big cats, give birth to the most cubs - up to five or six. Before we started filming *Big Cat Live* Shakira had six cubs.
**Opposite:** Lion cubs are so tiny when they are first brought out into the open and introduced to the rest of the pride at around eight weeks old that it is a miracle any survive.

For the first time in the history of *Big Cat* we would not be featuring the Marsh Lions. They were experiencing one of those periods of transition that every pride endures at times. But Simon and our producers had done their homework, identifying the Ridge Pride as the best group to concentrate on. There were two fine-looking pride males, at least four adult females and four feisty adolescents. The key characters, though, were two male cubs, Sala and Cheza. Sala was about two months old and cute as they come, while Cheza was around seven months and more than happy to lead the way. Sala was fearless and the worry was that he would end up getting himself into trouble with hyenas or other lions. He would provide the perfect mix of an engaging character facing real jeopardy.

Trouble wasn't long in coming, though not in the form of other predators. Once again it was the buffaloes – lots of them – who were making life difficult for the lions. The Ridge Pride often lie up in the middle of the day in a island of bush and rocks in the heart of their territory, to the south of Rhino Ridge. Our sequence shows that the buffaloes can smell the lions but can't yet see them – not until Cheza loses his nerve and runs. Sala is there too, standing on a track at the edge of the thicket. Suddenly he finds himself isolated. A lioness holds her ground as the buffaloes move closer, allowing both cubs the chance to escape. It looks almost inevitable that she will be killed, but somehow she manages to break through the press of animals while Sala tucks himself away among the rocks and bushes: 'If he is caught in the open he will be trampled, horned and crushed to death.'

It is getting dark and the crew have to head home. Next morning they are back before sunrise, fearful for the cubs' safety. They find one of the lionesses searching and calling. Cheza is with her. Eventually, much to Simon's delight and relief, Sala emerges from his hiding place under a rock where he has spent a cold and lonely night. He is none the worse for his adventure and receives a welcome lick on the head from his mother.

Nothing, it seems, can diminish the tenacious spirit of this little cub. He is growing fast and has already started to join his larger relatives at kills and to eat meat. He is familiar with every member of his extended family and feels totally at ease. As the pride gather together one morning, Sala puts on quite a performance, taking the liberty of tussling with one of the pride males as he lies on his side: clambering up onto backs, biting tails and generally being a pest is all part of being a cub. Males can be grumpy in such circumstances, but on this occasion the old boy seems oblivious to the little cub's games. As Simon says, 'Lions prides are very often a loose assembly of animals. It's not often you see them all come together like this. It really is quite a treat.' Then follows a delightful moment as one of the males begins to roar. Soon the whole pride are adding their distinctive voices to the chorus – even little Sala seems caught up in the moment, strutting around, squawking and yeowing in empathy with the rest of his pride: 'You've got to start somewhere,' Simon ventures.

The mood, though, can change as quickly as the weather out on the plains. Lions respond with brutal simplicity at times, showing no mercy when the stakes are high and they need to bring order to their world. Nowhere is this more clearly illustrated than when early one morning Simon and the lion team come upon two adult lionesses they don't know feeding on a wildebeest kill. The four adolescents from the Ridge Pride hover around them, hungry and eager to feast, but unsure of their reception. One of the older lionesses reacts with hostility to their approach, lunging and snarling to make them keep their distance. But the tables soon turn in the youngsters' favour as two adult lionesses from their own pride stalk towards the kill and chase away one of the older females, who appear to be outsiders. Suddenly it is six to one in favour of the Ridge Pride, but the dispute is far from over, making a dramatic ending to Programme 3.

Simon is in the thick of it, describing the drama as 'like watching a very slow-motion game of chess,

only here checkmate will either be very serious
injury or perhaps even death'. The beating inflicted
on the older female is protracted and merciless.
At times the attackers pause and lie down,
encircling their victim and preventing her from
running off. Everything goes quiet for a while and
if you didn't know better you might think this was
a tranquil scene. But whenever the old lioness
moves or tries to break away the confrontation
starts all over again, with the mob circling,
challenging her face to face, allowing others to close
in behind her, biting and clawing at her rump and
legs. Salivating profusely from fear, stress and her
attempts to keep cool in the burning heat, the old
lioness is eventually allowed to slink away as her
tormentors lose interest. A few days later Simon
catches up with her again: battered and barely
able to walk, she is a pathetic sight to behold.

**Above:** For a leopard independence is a gradual process. At 15 months Chui still sometimes shared his mother's kills; he wouldn't stake out a territory of his own and breed until he was at least three to four years old.

**Opposite:** Bella and Chui high up in a strangler fig tree, whose wide branches make it a favourite resting place, until the ripening figs attract troops of baboons to make the leopards' life uncomfortable.

On a happier note there is great excitement for the leopard team when one of the spotters locates a youngish female resting in the shade of a tree not far from where they last saw Bella. Might it be Chui's missing sister? Though it seems highly unlikely, Saba isn't about to take any chances and checks her records. The leopard is a real beauty,

with perfectly rounded ears – no nicks or cuts – and a rather narrow face with green, almond-shaped eyes that turn up slightly at the corners. She has a distinctive W of black spots over the bridge of her nose. The drivers tell us that she shares part of Bella's home range, and later Paul Karui, a highly experienced guide from Mara

Intrepids Camp, confirms that this is Chui's *older* sister, Olive, who is now four-and-a-half years old – the same leopard we had briefly filmed with her mother in 2000.

Chui meanwhile is up to all kinds of adventures, stalking up on crocodiles and teasing buffaloes. He is by turns cocky and playful, reckless yet wary – at heart still a cub but aware of the necessity for caution, as Saba points out: 'He needs to learn to give other predators a seriously wide berth.' Her words of warning are almost prophetic. Shortly after Bella has killed a zebra foal, both our leopards are treed by lions, with one lioness trying to climb the tree in which they have taken refuge. By some miracle the lions fail to find Bella's kill and she later hoists it into a tree. But Chui is taking no chances and remains where he is for some while before plucking up the courage to join his mother to feast. Later still, when Bella and Chui are more relaxed, Gordon Buchanan captures some lovely images of mother and son wrapped in each other's paws, playing.

Meanwhile our cheetah youngsters are pushing their luck in their attempts to find sufficient food. They have moved beyond the reserve boundary and we see them walking straight towards a large herd of livestock against the menacing backdrop of a dark, brooding sky. This is beautiful country, with clear views all the way to the Serengeti, the blue shapes of the Kuka Hills sharply profiled against the southern horizon. So far the cheetahs have managed to find sufficient natural prey to satisfy their hunger, but all the big cats sometimes succumb to the temptation to steal a sheep or goat or, in the case of a lion, a cow. Such bravado may be their only option if game is scarce or they are old or injured, but it might cost them their life, as Half-Tail's death had proved. But you have to be fair to the herdsmen: 'Believe me,' I say, 'the Masai have no quarrel with predators. They do their best to keep their livestock well away.' Our cheetahs might simply be being curious, but it is a game that could have deadly consequences.

# How big cats hunt

**B**ella and Kike generally look for prey smaller than themselves, though with some spectacular exceptions in Bella's case. Leopards and cheetahs must be careful not to get injured unnecessarily – they may die if they cannot hunt and feed themselves. At least a leopard can scavenge, as we see when Bella and Chui take advantage of a dead wildebeest right out in the open: 'It just shows how clever Bella is, because she will make the most of any opportunity that is presented to her, but she has to spend a lot of energy in just acquiring meals for herself and Chui. When you find good fresh meat like this, then why not just take it?' Cheetahs rarely do this; they rely on kills they have made for themselves. Being social, a pride of lions can tackle far larger creatures such as buffaloes, giraffes and elands, though when zebra or wildebeest are in the area they prefer to concentrate their efforts on these prey animals. Lions also have a safety net if they sustain an injury and times are tough; as long as they can limp to a kill made by members of their pride they are pretty much assured of their share of the food – if the kill is big enough.

The following morning we are relieved to find the three youngsters still looking hungry and moving back towards the reserve. The air of uncertainty and vulnerability that was so apparent when we first found them is beginning to wane. They have lived independently from Kike for the past three months, kept watch for lions and hyenas, been chased from their kill by baboons. Now they need to eat. Suddenly one of the females takes off in pursuit of a full-grown male impala, closing quickly to snag the antelope with her dew-claw. But large prey such as this does not give up easily and for a while the young cheetahs struggle to subdue it. Instead of immediately applying the throat hold they have practised with their mother, they cling to the impala's head and flanks, narrowly avoiding being skewered by those long, lyre-shaped horns as they grapple for the right hold. Finally one of them gets a secure grip and pulls the impala off its feet while another strangles it. They seem oblivious to the Masai herdsmen who watch from the edge of their thorn-rimmed boma as they prepare to release their livestock out on to the rain-washed plains.

**Opposite:** Cheetahs try to get close to their prey before launching a chase: they cannot sustain their amazing top speed for long.
**Above:** It takes a long time for young cheetahs to perfect the art of killing prey. Here, Duma, aged 14 months, struggles with a Grant's gazelle.

Whenever it pours all of us scramble to zip up the waterproof covers sealing our open camera doors. For our predators rain offers the chance to sneak up on prey. Saba watches as Bella moves in: 'It's an opportunity she won't be able to resist. The senses of the wildebeest will be muted by the storm.' We see the wily leopard easing herself out of a tree in full view of the wildebeest, but none of them spot her – they are too busy feeding, heads bowed as if in supplication. There is no wind to give Bella away, and plenty of long grass to conceal her approach. But it is still a risky move – out in the grassland she could be ambushed by lions. In the end her efforts to get close are to no avail: there are no calves, just bulls, and Bella walks away again. 'No point in wasting energy for no reward,' comments Saba.

The vast majority of the wildebeest manage to escape the attention of predators, partly by migrating, which is the only way they can gather in such unbelievable numbers – the chances of any one animal becoming a victim are greatly reduced. But predators are opportunistic, always ready to take advantage of an easy meal, a sick or injured animal. Simon watches as one of the lionesses from the Ridge Pride stalks towards a single wildebeest that has become separated from the anonymity of the herd. It is hobbling around on a badly lacerated leg. As the lioness closes in the wildebeest turns to defend itself, keeping her at bay. But not for long. Another lioness soon approaches, with Simon commenting, 'This is where co-operative hunting really pays off.' Surrounded, the end for the stricken beast is a foregone conclusion and the lions know it.

The dry season is drawing to a close and it will soon be time for the herds to head south again, back to the Serengeti Plains where the cow wildebeest give birth during the rainy season. Dramatic images of vast numbers of animals

funnelling away beneath a storm-black sky fill the television screen.

A rainbow emerges from the darkness. Saba picks up the mood: 'The storm seems to have passed and at last the clouds have parted, giving me a few final golden moments with Bella and Chui. For some reason Bella has let me into her world.' Bella is in her prime, while her son, who is almost the same size as her by now, is a mix of mischievousness and curiosity, gaining experience by the day as to how to survive on his own. We watch him with a porcupine stashed in a tree and can only imagine that he must

have captured this prickly customer for himself; eating it is probably not much easier than killing it. As Saba says: 'He's such a great character, I'm absolutely sure he's going to do fine.'

Simon feels equally confident about Sala's prospects of survival: Solo managed to make it through the wet season, so why not Sala? If the two ageing males can keep their pride intact he has a chance. The uncertainty of what might happen next is all part of the drama – we can never be sure what lies in store for our star cats. That is what keeps us coming back.

**Opposite:** Lions can go for long periods without drinking, but only if they conserve moisture by staying cool: this is one of the reasons they hunt mainly at night. They do not have many sweat glands and must pant to keep cool - a process called evaporative cooling. This young lioness is White Eye, before she lost her right eye and was given her name!

**Left:** A single balanites tree dwarfed by the grey thundery sky. The rains breathe new life into the Mara, renewing the plants and the woodlands.

## The week that was...

One thing is for certain, though: 'What adventures we've shared with our three cheetah youngsters during *Big Cat Week*.' They have met all the challenges the Mara has thrown at them — lions, hyenas, the risk of tackling large prey when still relatively inexperienced. In a few months they will split up, but if I meet them again I'll certainly recognise them. They have done Kike proud.

It's *Big Cat Week 3* and we're as keen as ever to find ways to move the brand forward. This year the innovation comes courtesy of the team working on *Planet Earth*, the pioneering high-definition natural-history series first broadcast by the BBC in 2006. A deal has been struck whereby we provide the *Planet Earth* team with accommodation in the *Big Cat* Camp and they record us a couple of hours of spectacular aerials. So at one point we see the chopper swooping low alongside me as I drive towards Paradise Plain, then soaring like a giant vulture, capturing everything for miles around. Suddenly there is a sense of scale and grandeur – a bird's-eye view of a solitary vehicle racing across the plains, a tiny dot in the wilderness.

# Spirit of
# Survival

This year it will be a young cheetah who has our audience on the edge of their seats. At the top of Programme 1 I name the cub Toto, meaning 'child' or 'little one' in Swahili, and little he most certainly is, small enough to fit in the palms of my hands. He is adorable, a tiny ball of fur with the long fluffy mantle of grey hair along his neck and back that is such a characteristic of very young cheetah cubs and helps to conceal them in the long grass. Toto goes everywhere with his mother, who later turns out to be none other than Honey. At the time, however, we don't know this, which is why we refer to her simply as Toto's mum.

In the meantime, Simon has been happily reunited with his old friends the Marsh Pride. Since last year, two new males have taken over the pride, but a few months ago one of them was attacked and killed by three powerful males from Paradise Plain. The Marsh Lions now consist of the lone pride male Notch, four lionesses and eight cubs from three or four different litters. All the cubs are under a year old when we start filming; the youngest, a little female called Moja (meaning 'one' in Swahili), is about three months.

Notch is in his prime, his nose still predominantly pink, peppered with a few black spots. But a single pride male is always vulnerable to a takeover bid. Just before we start filming our spotters locate two young males trespassing in and around the Marsh Pride territory: Notch is going to have a battle on his hands to maintain his tenure and ensure the safety of his cubs, mirroring events we witnessed with Simba two series ago. The question that we hope will provide a storyline for Simon is, will Notch be able to hold his own or will he be forced to capitulate to the young nomads and abandon his pride to their fate?

And what of the leopards? Saba has the toughest job of all. Everyone is hoping that Bella might have a new litter of cubs to enthral us with. Although it soon becomes apparent that this is not the case, the good news is that Bella's son Chui – now over two years old, old enough to live on his own – is still sometimes associating with her, particularly when she has made a sizeable kill. There is a lovely moment for Saba when she finds Bella and Chui together, allowing cameraman Gordon Buchanan to work his magic. We see Chui wind himself sinuously around his mother, pressing up against her, laying his beautiful spotted tail over her back and caressing her with it, playful and solicitous in the way that all young cats are when they want something – and that something is invariably food. Chui knows from his mother's smell that she has killed and later Bella leads him to the place where she has stashed her prey high up in the branches of a tree, allowing him to eat his fill.

Chui is a magnificent young animal, already larger than his mother, with signs of the massive broad head that is a defining feature of adult male leopards. Despite his adolescent ways there are hints of his impending independence. He sprays his individual odour on to bushes, letting his father, the dominant male in the area, know that he is still in residence.

**The numbers game**
Most prides in the Mara are accompanied by two males; larger coalitions like this group of Notch's younger relatives (see Chapter 9) can more easily dominate an area, sometimes controlling more than one pride territory.

Toto and Honey. As a single cub Toto's whole life was based around his mother.

The relationship between the presenters and the individual cats is by now as intimate as we can make it. When Notch is confronted by the two young nomads, you can see the tension reflected in Simon's eyes, hear it in his voice. Notch flaunts his black mane like a banner, his eyes blazing with a mixture of fear and hostility: he is ready to fight these intruders if they dare to stand their ground in the heart of his territory. And on that cliff-hanging note the first programme of the week comes to a dramatic end. Who wouldn't want to know what happened next?

The following morning Simon can discover no sign of the nomads, but he does track down Notch, looking none the worse for his encounter. In fact the lion has found himself a girlfriend – or perhaps she has found him. At this stage we don't know who she is or where she comes from, but she is in flirtatious mood, encouraging then coy. Notch has seen this all before: the female crouches in front of him, wafting her scent in his face, lashing her tail like a bull whip. She is not yet fully in oestrus – if she were, the two would mate: instead, she rolls on her back as if trying to rid herself of an insatiable itch. She is young, she doesn't yet have the thickset bearing of the older females in the pride, and this may well be her first oestrus. She has a narrow face with almond eyes set close

Rubbing heads is a friendly greeting among all cats

together, almost squinty. But she is beautiful too, destined to become the star act of the next series. We call her Tamu, which is Swahili for 'sweet'.

We leave the lions in order to catch up with Toto. He is a real character, whether wrestling with a gazelle carcass or playing with his mother. The ruff of long hair along his neck and back is still very pronounced, so he is probably no more than two months old, with a comical pug-face. When Honey is successful in a breathtaking chase after gazelles she turns back in Toto's direction and calls. The little cub races towards her, cheeping like a bird, and Honey responds with a stuttering churring call of encouragement. The relationship between mother and cub is strengthened by these events: the brief moments of play, the hunting for food to provide for her cub – all of this helps reaffirm the bond that attaches mothers to their young. Staying in contact with his mother is vital if Toto is to survive. For Honey her investment in her latest litter has now come down to this one tiny scrap of life.

It is this same bond that Bella is now in the process of breaking with

Chui. Leopards are so different to cheetahs, though. Separation is more gradual for these secretive cats, with young leopards at times wandering off on their own and hunting for themselves, taking small creatures such as hares and hyrax before graduating to larger prey such as gazelles and impalas. A young leopard can learn to survive like this on its own, but not a cheetah – a cheetah must stay with its mother until it can live permanently alone. The severing of the bond between mother and cubs is sudden and complete – they rarely reunite.

As for the lions, Notch may have managed to see off the challenge of the nomads but he now finds himself in hot water from a different quarter. The Marsh Pride females have tracked him down and the minute they see Tamu they give chase, while Notch attempts to keep her within touching distance. Right now his loyalties to his pride are secondary to his urge to mate.

But the four lionesses are equally determined to chase the young female from the perennial heart of their territory, roaring out a warning to her to move on.

Little Moja – the youngest cub in the Marsh Pride – with two older relatives. Once she is weaned, she will have to compete with them for food.

# bigcat diary

## Behind the
### scenes

# Making the stories **work**

A year earlier and just a week before we were due to finish filming we had come upon a mother cheetah with a single female cub of around the same age that Toto was now. We were all captivated by her and desperate to feature her in the programme. But series producer Nigel Pope rightly decided that this would weaken our story with Kike's cubs, and that it was too late for anything but a cameo role for Duma (meaning 'cheetah' in Swahili), as she became known. But once filming finished Angie and I stayed on for a week or so to follow and photograph Duma. We didn't know her mother well enough to have given her a name at that point, but later, as Shakira, she would become another of our stars.

By now – 2005 – Duma was almost as large as her mother and at 14 months old nearing independence (in fact later in the series mother and cub did part company, much to Duma's initial distress). We decided to film Duma as a way of illustrating the fact that, despite all the dangers facing young Toto, it was possible for a single cub to survive to independence – that there was hope. And if Toto didn't make it we would have established another cheetah character that we could follow.

*When you spend 14 hours a day in your car it's good to take a break!*

Interspersed with the stories of our big cats there was ample opportunity to celebrate life in the Mara; there is such a variety of habitats and species that we were always spoiled for choice. The wild oscillations in the weather provided plenty of excitement and drama of their own. There were times when it was blisteringly hot; others when it poured with rain, generating some memorable scenes: the eight lion cubs gambolling about in the deluge, with the older ones unable to resist playing with little Moja; and Bella hunting in the rain, creeping towards a herd of gazelles, totally focused as her quarry stood hunched with their backs to the wind and rain.

Shakira with her cub Duma, aged three months. By the time we found these two captivating cheetahs, it was too late to include them in our story. But Duma was proof that a single cub could survive to maturity.

**Constant vigilance**
A cheetah mother must always be on the look-out when feeding, particularly when there are vultures around, to alert lions or hyenas to her presence. If she spots danger she growls, prompting her cubs to run.

**A**ll of us knew that at some point during our month-long shoot we would be faced with a dilemma. What do you do when an animal such as Toto is under threat? Do you intervene on the cub's behalf? That moment arrived when two male baboons appeared on the scene, attracted to Honey's kill by the vultures hovering overhead. By chance, my DV director Toby Strong asked me the day before what I would do if such an occasion arose. By this time all of us had become enchanted by the cheetah cub, so Toby couldn't quite believe it when I said without hesitation that I would let nature take its course. He was visibly upset and insisted that we ask Warren Samuels what he would do. Warren's answer was the same as mine: he would film whatever took place; that was his job as a wildlife cameraman.

In the programme, we see Honey respond immediately to the danger posed by the baboons, walking towards them with her head lowered in threat, trying to lead them away from her cub. Toto flees for his life, then stops and calls for his mother, a potentially suicidal instinct on his part, underlining just how vulnerable he is.

I turn to camera, conscious of my conversation with Toby: 'You cannot intervene, it's just not fair – but your heart is crying out.' I believed that. But I had gone to bed the previous evening thinking about what Toby had said, questioning whether or not I had to act as I had said I would. Is there another option – I am human, after all; surely it is only natural to want to try to save the life of another creature? But we can't play God: nature has its own rules and we have to respect them.

One thing is certain, there is no need to look for a dramatic ending to this programme – we have a real-life cliff-hanger for our audience.

In the end Honey's tactics of first letting the baboons know she is there, then trying to distract them and keeping a cool head pay off. Toto crouches in the grass as one of the baboons moves closer. It sits plucking at the fresh green leaves that have sprung up in the wake of the rains. After what seems like an eternity it gets up and moves away. Once it is safe to approach, Honey walks carefully towards the patch of grass where Toto lies hidden, bends down and acknowledges the cub's existence with the most cursory of licks. It is an incredibly powerful piece of television, full of all the emotions that one faces in these heart-rending moments. By the end of the series Toto's name is on everyone's lips.

Honey was one of the most successful cheetah mothers in the Mara, raising nearly half her cubs – a remarkable achievement.

# A case of very **bad** timing

One of the elements of *Big Cat* that people love is following individual cats from one series to the next. So we were delighted when Angie spotted Kike accompanied by a male. This almost certainly meant that she was in oestrus and ready to mate, something that you rarely witness with cheetahs. Kike made a bee line for Warren's camera car, leaping up on to the canvas awning that acted as a sunshade over his camera door. We chuckled as Warren desperately tried to keep the awning from collapsing like a soggy umbrella into his arms. After a while she took the hint and settled down on the roof, much to the chagrin of the male cheetah, who stood with his front paws up against the spare wheel, perplexed and frustrated. He obviously wasn't one of those cheetahs who had learned to climb on to vehicles as a cub and he wasn't about to start now.

Eventually Kike jumped down and rolled on the ground in front of the young male, who looked inexperienced around an oestrus female. We waited all day for the courting couple to mate until, desperate for a pee, Warren and I moved away for a moment, leaving Angie to keep watch. Just as we were relieving ourselves Angie called on the radio to say the cheetahs were about to mate. We scrambled back into our vehicles, but it was too late – copulation in cats is brief at the best of times – and we missed the shot. Next time we needed to pee we would definitely use an empty water bottle!

Kike disappeared sometime in 2006, shortly after losing her latest cubs: she failed to raise another litter after the success of 2003/2004. When we last saw her she looked old and was in poor health; she was later treated for mange, but never recovered her full strength. It was a sad end for our star cheetah.

Scenically, the Talek area where Bella lives really lends itself to photography. It's a beautiful mosaic of grasslands broken by patches of croton bush and bisected by the winding course of the river with its slabs of grey stone and the distinctive silhouettes of giant fig trees. The river is the heart of Bella's territory, somewhere she can hide her cubs and ambush prey, a retreat from the prying eyes of visitors when they press too close, and a safe refuge from the prides of lions that also covet this place. You always expect her to emerge suddenly from cover – and rejoice when she does. You can almost hear the rush of adrenalin Saba is experiencing as a herd of wildebeest mass along the river bank, crammed together so tightly that they can barely move. Startled, they stampede away as Bella rushes in behind them, closing within easy reach of the stragglers. Surely this time she must succeed. But she hesitates; they are all adults and she is hoping for a calf.

When Bella finally makes a kill that we can film it is a huge relief for all of us and there is a good deal of celebrating on the way home to camp that night. Not only has Bella managed to secure a meal for herself, she has provided us with one of the most dramatic hunts of the entire series. Her target is a small group of male Thomson's gazelles gathered at the edge of the river. The first gazelle crosses safely,

*Of all the big cats, leopards are the most volatile. Disturb one at your peril!*

Bella struggled to raise another litter after Chui became independent. There are lots of lions and hyenas along the Talek River, and always the threat of infanticide from male leopards.

but as the second trots up the bank Bella launches herself like a missile down the slope, forcing the gazelle to flee back along the bank and into the water. In a last desperate attempt to escape it catapults out of the water again, only to slam head first into a wall of rock with a sickening thud before falling back into the river once more. Not to be denied, Bella immediately disappears under the water, grabbing the stunned gazelle by the throat and hauling it backwards up the slippery grassy bank.

Water is becoming something of a theme for our cats. There is a delightful scene as the Marsh Pride gather at one of their favourite midday resting places – the lake-sized pit close to

Governor's Camp airstrip which was dug to provide murram to surface the runway. The pit is a scenic stop-off for visitors eager to watch the hippos and waterbirds such as jacanas and egrets that gather here. Fascinated by the birds, a dozen lions peer down over the steep bank. Simon can see what is likely to happen next and is having a good chuckle when 'oops' – sure enough, one of the smallest cubs leaps down on to what it thinks is solid ground, only to disappear under the moveable carpet of vegetation. Seconds later the cub emerges, spluttering in distress as it doggy-paddles to the edge, failing abysmally in its initial attempts to scramble back up the bank. Thank goodness for those clawed paws. On its second attempt and driven on by sheer panic the cub manages to grapple its sodden little body back on to dry land as the rest of the pride look on with a mixture of fascination and bemusement.

131

I love the drive out onto the plains each morning: emerging from the darkness of the forest edges bordering the Mara River where we camp, revelling in the mist that hangs like a giant silken cobweb over the marsh. On and up over Rhino Ridge, always pausing for a moment to check with binoculars in case Honey has moved further north. No sign of our cheetah family as I crest the rise, but then the radio suddenly crackles into life: our spotter Chris Brennan is calling to say that, while he has yet to find Toto and Honey, the Paradise males are on the prowl. A brooding sense of danger now looms across the plains. There is something primeval about the scene; these great warrior beasts patrolling their domain, roaring to proclaim their presence and their right to this land. Watching the tapes years later I listen as the music kicks in. This was a moment of real danger – I knew at the time that these males would kill Toto given the chance, and I can feel it again now.

The tension is almost unbearable as the three lions walk single file towards what we call Toto's Hill, a low rocky rise with a crown of dense croton bushes: this is a place Honey has often chosen as a night-time refuge for herself and her cub. At one point the males stop and stare into the thickets and I hold my breath, certain that they have spotted Honey and Toto. But the suspense is finally broken as a lioness appears from the bushes and greets them – it is the Paradise Pride, not the cheetahs.

Little wonder then that when we next catch up with Honey and Toto they are ready to move on. But wherever Honey goes there will always be danger. The soundtrack mirrors the emotion, the tribal voices of Africa heightening the despair we are all feeling. Some people said afterwards that we were manipulating viewers' emotions. That simply wasn't true – this was a rollercoaster of a ride for all of us.

Honey heads east towards a ridge overlooking a beautiful plain with a prominent hill that we have named Duma's Hill, after the young female cheetah we have been following: there are plenty of gazelles and impalas here for a cheetah to hunt. But this is also a cheetah graveyard. Duma's mother Shakira has lost cubs here in the past; the area is riddled with rocky hideaways where we have often found lions, hyenas and leopards.

Despite all the drama with the cheetahs, over in the marsh Simon is struggling with the lion story. There are characters he can identify with, such as White Eye with her one blind eye and Red (our new name for Mama Lugga), who is the star hunter in the pride and often the first to react to trouble; and the eight cubs are certainly a joy to watch when they are in playful mood or getting up to mischief. But the two nomadic males who looked as if they might make life uncomfortable for Notch earlier on in the series have disappeared, and with them has gone any sense of jeopardy. Notch remains unchallenged and the pride are being typical lions – they just aren't doing very much during daylight hours.

The pride has recently moved in to the marsh in their search for food, with Red leading the way. Closing like a noose around an unsuspecting wart hog – the staple diet for smaller groups of lionesses when food is scarce – they finally make a kill, and while three of the adult females battle over the spoils the fourth goes off to fetch the cubs from a patch of shady trees in the centre of the marsh. But a kill this size won't satisfy the pride for long and the scene quickly degenerates into a bellicose brawl for possession of the scraps.

Saba and the leopard crew are having difficulties too. Whenever they find Bella, as often as not she simply melts into the undergrowth, sometimes for hours at a time, all day even, leaving the crew frustrated and tired, sweating in the heat for fear of leaving the place where she has last been seen. When Bella does finally kill a topi, she goes and finds Chui and leads him to it. But it isn't long before lions steal the kill, which is too heavy for Bella to drag in to a tree; they chase her away and at last provide Saba with a moment of real drama.

With only a few days left for filming, the heavens open. This means damp beds and muddy tracks, a struggle simply to keep the vehicles moving along the treacherously slippery road leading away from camp. When we find Honey and Toto they are trying to shelter from the rain but there is nowhere to hide and the little cub crouches soaked to the skin and shivering with cold as he tries to bury himself under his mother's legs. The following morning there is no sign of either of them. We call on the lion and leopard crews to help in the search, but despite all our efforts – nothing. It is if our cheetahs had never existed.

The rains bring the wildebeest flooding back into the Marsh Pride's territory and at last the lions deliver. It is a long and exciting chase. Eventually in desperation the bull wildebeest turns and faces its attacker, lowering its head to try to horn the lioness who is leading the onslaught. But she is too wily for that, rolling onto her back and reaching up to grab the bull by the neck. Now there will be plenty of food for all the cubs.

I drive down to a crossing point on the Talek River, still searching for Toto. The river has receded sufficiently for me to cross – and if I can do it, so can the cheetahs. We speak to the drivers from all the other camps but, although everyone is looking, no one has seen them. There are the inevitable false alarms and disappointments – we find a mother with a single cub the same age as Toto, but she has an ear tag, so we know it can't be Honey.

## A sorrowful note

By now we have run out of time, and I must draw a line under events for our audience: 'Two days after we left the Mara we received news from Simon and his wife Marguerite, who had stayed on to film a sequence on cheetahs for *Planet Earth*, that Honey had been found — but without little Toto. We'll never know what happened, but the odds were always stacked against him. It's harsh out here and these are real-life dramas — inevitably for some of our cats there just can't be a happy ending.'

# Jeopardy
## on the Plains

The question most people wanted to ask me after the last series was, 'What happened to Toto? Have you found him yet?' Some even volunteered to come out to Kenya to help in the search. Might he not still be alive? Sadly it would be impossible for a cub barely three months old to survive without his mother. When Honey reappeared shortly after we finished filming there was only one conclusion: Toto had died.

But it isn't all bad news for Honey. During the early part of 2006 she gave birth to five cubs in the Mara Triangle, basing herself for a while on the plains just to the south of Kichwa Tembo, within 1 km (½ mile) or so of Little Governor's. Angie and I kept track of the family through our network of drivers and guides: when the cubs were about three months old one of them disappeared and we waited with bated breath, knowing how delighted our viewers would be to find that Honey had cubs again.

For the cheetah team this would mean following the same routine that Simon had adopted four years earlier, parking our vehicles at Little Governor's each night and using the ferry.

# big Cat diary

# Who is Tamu?

The older lionesses in the Marsh Pride made life tough for Tamu

Tamu's union with Notch had failed to yield cubs – either that or they had died – but the pair had mated again and at the start of the 2006 series Tamu had four tiny cubs of six to eight weeks old in tow. Our hunch was that she was one of the two young females who used to hang out with Nusu Nusu and the young male Kijana – the ones we had seen four years earlier disturbing Mama Lugga and her first litter of cubs. That would explain the age difference between the older females in the Marsh Pride, who were eight years old, and Tamu, who was around four. Also, Tamu was in excellent physical condition – groups of lionesses often beat up strangers who invade their territory, and she showed no signs of this, which made it likely that she was a relative.

Wherever she came from, Tamu lived on the fringes of the Marsh Pride – like Bibi, she seemed to be the only surviving female of her age group – and we knew from watching Bibi's struggles two years earlier that Tamu would have an uphill battle to keep her cubs alive. It wasn't impossible – Bibi was eventually reintegrated into the nurturing fold of the pride and her cubs survived – but it was certainly going to provide us with the jeopardy our producers craved.

As the series begins, we are in high spirits at the thought of spending time with our favourite cheetah: Angie is spotting for the cheetah crew again, as well as taking the publicity photographs for the series, and Japhet Kivango is with us too. Cameraman Warren Samuels and his driver Wilson Wemali are also important figures. Rounding off the team is Chris Brennan, who helps co-ordinate our efforts and logs Honey's position each day on his GPS. This is just as well. Honey is a bit of a nomad, moving widely with her cubs, who are now about six months old. There is a time when she heads south for the Serengeti and we fear we may lose her before the end of the series.

We all love working in the Triangle, not just because it is such beautiful country but because there is less traffic and tighter controls on tourism, with a vehicle called Cheetah One, funded by *Big Cat Diary* and by Angie and me, to keep an eye on drivers to ensure that they don't crowd a cheetah mother when she is trying to hunt. We are delighted to see how effective this is proving to be: most people play by the rules and are rewarded with some extraordinary encounters with Honey and her cubs.

familiar enough to the drivers to have been given names: he is either Big Boy or another bruiser known colourfully as Golden Balls. It seems that Bella is holding court near the boundary between at least two of these males' territories, so even though it is difficult to see what is going on among the bushes the sounds are pretty descriptive – roars, rumbles, growls and snarls mixed with the unmistakable caterwauling of mating. It is quite a performance, sadly conducted in the shadows of deep cover for which the Talek is well known and one reason why it is such a good area for leopards.

Honey's cubs are already large and nimble enough to jump up on to the spare wheels of Warren's camera vehicle. They are quite a handful by this age and Honey is going to have her work cut out to feed them and keep them safe. But with the migration streaming into the Triangle, it must gladden the heart of an experienced hunter like Honey to see all those wildebeest calves galloping alongside their mothers, or better still to spot one that has been orphaned – a straggler that will be easy to pick off without a mother to defend it. The long stands of red oat grass are a bonus, too, helping to conceal Honey from a mother wildebeest whenever she brings down a calf. Cows can be ferocious in defence of their young, but are confused and unsure of what they are facing when a predator is concealed by tall grass. Honey knows this – it is part of her strategy.

As luck would have it, just as Honey hits top gear my vehicle decides to throw a wobbly – the starter solenoid refuses to kick in. Cursing my luck I leap out of the car and raise the bonnet, give the starter a hefty smack and jump back in. To a cheer from the other occupants the engine explodes into life and we are off. But by then Honey has knocked her victim to the ground and is busy strangling it, fortunately all captured on tape by Warren. Once the calf is dead and Honey has checked to see if the stampeding herd has alerted unwanted company, she calls the cubs to join her. They are ravenous and quickly start to feed.

B ack in the Marsh Pride area, Simon also has a mother and cubs to work with: Tamu, the young lioness we saw mating with Notch last year (see box). But while Simon and I are fortunate to have our storylines sorted for us, Saba has the unenviable task of trying to track down Bella for the fourth year running. There is still no sign of cubs. It seems likely that Bella has lost at least one litter since giving birth to Chui and his sister three years ago. Leopard cub mortality is high in areas where there are so many lions and hyenas – up to 80 per cent die before maturity, and a mother

leopard often loses her entire litter before the cubs are even old enough to follow her as she moves around her home range. Chui has been one of the lucky ones: he is now fully independent and has established himself beyond his mother's territory.

The good news for our leopard team is that Bella is in oestrus: at one point our spotters locate four males in the area, all showing a keen interest, including one giant of an animal with a massive head and dewlap. Although he is shy – like so many male leopards – and difficult to identify positively, he is thought to be one of two males who are

**A real success story**
This was Honey's fourth litter that we knew of and by now she was seven or eight years old. Though cheetahs are said to live up to 20 years in captivity, few wild cheetahs reach half this age.

Tamu is less fortunate when she leaves her cubs to hunt. Who should she bump into but three young males from the Marsh Pride – Notch's sons or nephews – pumped full of testosterone and itching for a scrap. Tamu lies facing them as they strut sideways, almost crab-like, to make themselves look bigger and more

menacing. But the young lioness has been through this before and holds her ground. The males pause, unsure of themselves, rubbing heads with one another for reassurance, as if to say, 'You are with me, aren't you? You will back me up if this gets nasty? We are going to do this, right?' Finally they build up sufficient courage

seems surprisingly unconcerned. Is she making a fatal mistake or will her years of experience see her through?

Next morning the cheetah team are out before dawn. Angie radios to say she has spotted Honey moving about on the top of a low rocky hill not far from yesterday's kill, but she can see only three cubs. We are all dismayed – it's almost as if by posing the possibility that Honey might have been foolhardy the previous night we have somehow made it come true. After all the joy of watching Honey with a new litter, we feel gutted that she has lost a second cub just when it looked as if they were old enough to win through.

The news from the lion team lightens our mood. Tamu has been reunited with her cubs during the night. You can tell how relieved Simon is as he watches them, though he is under no illusions as to what the future might hold: 'Tamu, you're going to have to enjoy these moments of peace and quiet because you've got an uphill struggle ahead of you. So just keep your head down, keep those cubs hidden and look out for trouble.'

to charge, prompting Tamu to run for the river, driving her over the steep bank. The music soars, heightening the tension. What about Tamu's cubs? Will they be safe on their own? You can feel the jeopardy building as we race towards the close of the first programme.

To add to our concerns, Honey and the cubs are still out on the plains with their kill. We have stayed with them all day hoping that they will feed quickly and move on – that's what cheetahs are meant to do if they are to remain safe from larger predators. Now it is getting dark and we have to head back to camp. The lions and hyenas will soon be on the move, if they aren't already. Honey

Before you know it we are back with the cheetahs, the editors shaping the two stories in tandem, upping the pace, keeping the audience on the edge of their seats. Honey leads her cubs back to where she made the kill, calling, looking. She stops, sniffs, then crouches, hunched forward, burying her head in the long grass. She has found her lost cub. It is a horribly violent image, the little body torn and twisted. It has to be lions – hyenas would have eaten their victim. In the distance we see a male lion wandering away across the plains. Was it him? Did he catch the smell of a wildebeest carcass on the wind, creep forward unseen, then explode with that frightening turn of speed, the long grass impeding the cub's escape? It's the female cub who has died, leaving three brothers.

Almost before the audience has had time to absorb what has happened we are transported back across the river to where another drama is unfolding. Cut to Simon charging along in his vehicle – he is driving himself this series. One of our spotters has radioed to say that a big male lion has moved in on the Bila Shaka Lugga and it isn't Notch. The music throbs with anticipation; you know that whoever this male is he means business.

The tension is white hot as we cut again to Honey and the cubs. You can feel Honey's distress in her every move, see it in her large liquid eyes, hear it in her plaintive calls. But there is no time to mourn: life must move on. She turns and leads the cubs away. They have stopped calling now and hurry to keep up with their mother, anxious to turn their backs on the events of last night. Cut.

Simon has been joined by wildlife cameraman John Aitcheson: the two of them work together on *Springwatch* and John knows exactly what is required. He is a superb cameraman who can cover the action single-handed whenever Simon needs to commentate. None of us know who this male is but it's obvious that he is looking for Tamu's cubs. Simon's loyalties are with the young lioness: it's almost certainly her first litter and we all want her to succeed. Tamu knows something is wrong but tries to stay calm. Her cubs call out for her, then try to worm their way deeper into cover, perhaps sensing her concern. What is she to do? The male knows the cubs are here, he can hear them. He pauses, listening. This is his moment, this is what a male lion sometimes has to do in order to become a father. Simon is in no doubt: 'This is the body language of a cub killer right here.'

Cut to vervet monkeys chickering in alarm along the Talek River. It's Bella and she has finally finished mating. Saba manages to get a clear view of her: 'She's really beginning to show her age. She's still got teeth in excellent condition, but her ears are all ragged and she's beginning to lose the hair behind them. She's looking very lean and haggard.'

The audience love Bella, no question about that, but right now they want to know what is happening with the lions. The male is no more than 15 m (50 ft) from Tamu and moving forward. The footage is horrifying yet fascinating. For the viewer it conjures up the terrifying prospect of being stalked by a big cat. The male is almost on top of Tamu and the cubs – 180 kg (400 lb) of killing machine poised to strike. He lunges into the belly of the lugga, and grabs a cub by the chest. It cries out in pain and fear and in the same instant Tamu launches herself upwards and onto the male's back, mouth gaping wide in a terrifying snarl, aiming for his head. The male drops the cub and runs, with Tamu clawing at his heels. There are blood-curdling roars and growls, grunts and bellows, as Tamu drives him away before running back to her cubs.

Opposite: Tamu was constantly on the alert. She had to hunt for herself and try to keep her cubs safe, no easy task for a single lioness, particularly when she had constantly to avoid contact with the Marsh Pride – her relatives.
Right: Infanticide is a fact of life in lion society. By killing cubs sired by the previous pride males, new males are able to mate with the lionesses more quickly. A few days after White Eye lost her cubs in 2007, she was mating with the male who had killed them.

Simon is stunned by what he has just witnessed. He knows all about infanticide, but it is rarely seen and almost never filmed. He punches his fist in delight at the thought that Tamu has saved her cubs; his relief is palpable. 'Unbelievable, I thought for sure that he was going to come in and kill the cubs. Unbelievable, what a mum Tamu is.' What Simon doesn't realise yet is that from John's camera position the audience has watched the male grab one of the cubs before Tamu forces him to release it. Simon can't see this from where he is – he can only commentate on what he has witnessed, proving just how real it is for all of us out there – we tell it as we see it and tidy up the loose ends later. It is the immediacy that counts.

Left: Cubs are fascinated by an older relative's swishing tail – the perfect plaything to sink their needle-sharp teeth into.
Below: Notch, one of the most successful pride males we have followed, squaring up to one of his younger relatives.

The following day Simon watches as Tamu moves her cubs. She emerges from the lugga with two of them, one of which is hobbling along on an injured right leg. It is almost unbearable to watch: there is blood on the cub's chest where the male bit it. And where are the other two cubs? She started with four. Has there been another attack during the night – did the male return?

Simon puts what has happened into perspective: 'These things go on all the time all around us, you know, whether it is lions, cheetahs, leopards, wildebeest, elephants, zebras – their life-and-death struggles are playing out every single day here in the Mara. But they are so much more profound, so much more meaningful when you spend time watching the individuals, when you know them intimately, and it's hard to divorce yourself and say, well, I can't get involved. But we can't get involved, we can't play that role. That's not why we're here.'

It is not long before Tamu returns to the lugga to search for the missing cubs. But there is no sign of life from the croton thickets. When she returns to the place where she has left the other two cubs she finds the injured one has died. She sniffs at it while her surviving cub playfully bites at her leg.

Meanwhile, while Tamu seems to be losing the battle, Honey and her three boys are thriving, full of mischief and aggressive in their play, as might expect of males who, when they're older, will sometimes have to fight to defend a territory against other males: 'These three are going to boss, they're going to rule the area they settle in. It may not be right here, they'll probably move away from their mum's home range, but they will stick together for the rest of their lives. And why? Power in numbers, easier to hold a territory, easier to look out for danger, easier to hunt.' That doesn't stop their mother from once in a while letting them know who is boss – at least for the time being – pinning them to the ground or delivering a slap with a forepaw or a nip with her sharp teeth when they get too rowdy. She is also working overtime to feed her cubs, providing them with a mix of wildebeest, reedbuck and Thomson's gazelles. The cubs are learning by experience and when their mother grabs a young gazelle they are quick to seize on the opportunity: 'Let them actually tussle with the prey, let them pretend it's still alive, let them practise the bite in the throat, let them grab it and pull it because when they're adults they have to do that for themselves.'

Life moves on, sometimes in miraculous ways. Two days after the attack, Simon finds Tamu with two, then three cubs. There are tears in his eyes at the joyful discovery. None of us can quite believe it. But a lot goes on at night that we never witness; our big cats have their own ways of dealing with disaster. Has Tamu been visiting the two 'lost' cubs under cover of darkness, suckling them and then moving away, waiting for the right moment to reunite her family? If she had a strategy it has paid

handsome dividends. There is barely time for us to celebrate before Tamu takes the cubs – two males and a female – on a potentially dangerous trek to the marsh. She must try to stay clear of the rest of the Marsh Pride, but she must hunt too. Lone females often do this in the daytime, so they can stay with their cubs at night to protect them.

Meanwhile, the leopards are feasting; Saba finds a young female in a gardenia bush with a gazelle kill. There is a chance that it is Bella's daughter

Olive, who would now be six and a half years old, but it is difficult to see and we can't be sure. Meanwhile Bella is showing her adaptability, hunting topi, wildebeest, Thomson's gazelles, dik-dik and hares. But the lions and hyenas are everywhere, frequently driving her from her kills before she has managed to stash them safely in the trees. When it all gets too much for her at least *she* can seek refuge in one of the giant fig trees that are such a feature of the Talek River, leaving the lions and hyenas staring wistfully skywards.

Cut back to the marsh where, as we feared she might, Tamu is also having trouble with the neighbours. Simon reports: 'Oh, oh. Red from the Marsh Pride is making her way towards her and I don't think it's to invite her over for tea.' Red's body language seethes with aggression: she is determined to teach Tamu a lesson. Other members of the pride close in and it looks as if Tamu is going to take a beating until Notch swaggers over. He has defended her before – after all, she is the mother of his cubs. Things are always volatile in situations like this where loyalties are ambivalent. There is lots of noise and slapping, culminating in a mighty chorus of roars from the pride, but nothing worse than that.

Next morning Simon finds Tamu, but with only two cubs – the little female is missing. The lioness is hunkered down deep within the marsh: 'It's easy for Tamu to negotiate this land, but for those little guys every tussock is a hill, every termite mound is a mountain and every narrow ditch of water is a lake for them to cross. There are so many new things, so many new life experiences all piling in on top of each other.' At that point the lions very nearly bump into a hippo wallowing in the middle of the marsh, giving the cubs a shock. One of them then disappears out of its depth in a pool of water, emerging like a drowned rat and prompting Tamu to reach down to pull it out. But treacherous as it looks among the reedbeds, here at least mother and cubs can find shade and water with little chance of the cubs being discovered by the other lions.

### Under pressure

Leopards are the most numerous and adaptable of the big cats, ranging from Africa across Asia as far as Indonesia. But both distribution and numbers have shrunk in recent years due to pressure from humans.

# big Cat diary

## Cameramen at work

**W**hat made the sequence of Honey's confrontation with the lioness so powerful were the camera angles (see main text, right), Warren and Wilson managed to be virtually in two places at once, capturing both the lioness's head-on approach and Honey's viewpoint, pulling focus from one cat to the other. That took quick reactions and perfect timing; they had to think ahead so they knew exactly the right position for the camera. You need a deep understanding of an animal's behaviour in order to know exactly where to be, and when.

Warren – with Wilson's help – made a habit of this over the years: in 2008 he captured another awesome confrontation, this time between a male lion and Shakira. He followed this with his greatest coup: Honey's three cubs, by now big muscular adults, rising oh so menacingly from a termite mound and stalking shoulder to shoulder, heads held low, towards Shakira's cubs, then breaking into a intimidating run, flat out, to put the fear of God into the tiny cheetahs. It was pure theatre.

Over in the Triangle Honey and her family have suffered a fright during the night; two of the cubs have taken refuge high up in a balanites tree. It's a bit of a struggle for them to get down, but better than ending up in the stomach of the hyenas who were probably responsible for sending them scrambling for safety.

It is not over yet for the cheetahs, as they are spotted by a lioness with a look of menace in her eyes. But Honey is no stranger to confrontations with lions: we saw her defend her cubs when Simon was filming her in 2002. This lioness is in for a surprise. Honey's low growl of warning has already sent the cubs bolting away as she maintains her position between them and the lioness. You can see that the cheetah wants to slink away but the lioness is having none of it, so Honey decides to take the initiative, to get her response in first, galloping towards the startled lioness, who turns and runs. Honey quickly gains on her, slapping the ground with her forepaws for emphasis, something that you never see lions or leopards do. With their phenomenal speed and acceleration cheetahs are the masters of defensive aggression.

**O**ver at the marsh Tamu has a surprise for Simon as she emerges from her hiding place among the reeds. Much to his joy a third cub appears – it's the little female, the one we thought had been killed: 'I cannot tell you how happy that makes me feel – alone for a whole night surrounded by the rest of the pride – she is just the best mum.' Delightful scenes follow of Tamu and the three cubs gambolling about as she leads them to a kill. It is almost a miracle.

There is just time for me to wrap it up: 'The Masai Mara in Kenya never ceases to amaze me. For every animal on the plains each day is just a struggle to stay alive and big cats are no exception. Honey really is an incredible individual; we've seen just how difficult it is for a mother cheetah to raise her cubs… There are so many dangers out here it is no wonder so few cheetah cubs live to reach adulthood. But these three, well they've got a mum in a million teaching them the art of survival. When we come back in a year's time, maybe the cubs will still be with Honey. But maybe they will have taken their first steps to independence. I can hardly wait to see them.'

Little did I realise as I spoke these words what dramas there were going to be for Honey and her cubs — and for Big Cat Week — over the next two years.

bigcat diary
BIG CAT LIVE
2008

# End
## of an
# Era

Honey and her 'Boys' — she raised three of these cubs to independence

The cubs investigate the termite mound as Honey keeps a watchful eye

Honey died suddenly on the afternoon of 17 February 2007. It was a tragedy precipitated by a well-intentioned veterinary intervention. The *Big Cat* crew were not present to capture the incident – we always film around September – but I was at home in Nairobi when I received the news of her death.

**The right time to intervene**
The late Dr Zahoor Kashmiri and his team treat Honey and her four cubs for mange in April 2004. Mange is a skin mite that can be lethal and is often a sign of stress or poor health.

Cheetahs and wild dogs are known to be sensitive to anaesthetics and this may have played a part in Honey's demise, though there were also concerns about the fact that she was not placed in the shade immediately after being darted, nor 'wetted down' to help regulate her temperature – standard procedure for this kind of intervention.

The vet had been called in to treat one of Honey's cubs, who had injured his foot while scrambling up into a tree to escape from baboons. Honey had suffered superficial wounds in the same incident, so she was darted before the vet attempted to treat the cub. She almost immediately began to convulse. At some point the vet in charge treated her leg with an antibiotic spray, gave her the antidote to bring her round and placed her in the thicket where her family had been resting. She was still convulsing intermittently. The cub was then successfully darted, treated and put in a thicket to recover. By this time Honey had got to her feet, but seemed disoriented, and frightened by people moving around on foot. She uttered what were described as 'strange strangling sounds', similar to the noises she had made when first darted. She died later that afternoon.

Honey was no stranger to veterinary treatment. In 2004, when she and her four cubs developed mange, it was decided to treat the whole family, and I joined the late Dr Zahoor Kashmiri, who was at that time the vet of choice for this kind of intervention. All five cheetahs were anaesthetised, the skin encrustations removed and the animals treated for mange and given a long-lasting antibiotic. Honey was very disoriented when she came round – was this a sign of things to come? We waited for a few hours until she was reunited with her cubs and made sure she was all right before we left.

The following morning there was no sign of one of the cubs: it must have died or been killed during the night. Honey successfully raised the three remaining cubs and at some point crossed the river with them to roam around the Musiara area and Paradise Plain. These were the cubs who disappeared before we could film them (see Chapter 6).

A number of top BBC executives had come out to the Mara during the filming of *Big Cat Week* in the summer of 2006 and had been greatly impressed by our operation. Peter Fincham, the Controller of BBC1, was a big fan, but while *Big Cat* and the other 'Diaries' delivered excellent audience figures and approval ratings during the week they were broadcast, Peter was keen to commission a programme that could fill the 7 pm slot every day of the week, every week. This idea spawned *The One Show*, which has gone on to become a highly successful mix of current affairs, celebrity interviews and features on topics including British wildlife. But it also led to a protracted hiatus as the schedulers struggled to place the Diaries in a consistent time slot stripped across a single week. Consequently, series 4 of *Big Cat Week* – Tamu and Honey's story – which should have gone out in December 2006 or January 2007 sat on the shelf until January 2008, by which time Honey had been dead for almost a year. We couldn't help wondering if *Big Cat* might die with her.

Honey's four cubs were confined until they came round from the anaesthetic and the vet was happy they had suffered no ill effects. Sadly, the cub that had been most seriously affected by mange disappeared during the night, but the other three survived and separated from their mother just over a year later.

The *Daily Mail* printed a full-page story on the death of our star big cat. As a result, many people believed we had hidden the fact of Honey's death and somehow contradicted ourselves on the whole issue of intervening in the lives of wild animals. The fact is that in the Masai Mara Reserve it is an offence for the general public (and that includes the *Big Cat* team and other film-makers) to intervene to 'save' an animal from attack by a predator or rival – and on *Big Cat* we have always said that we cannot play favourites, however much we may long to when 'our' cats are in trouble. But it is up to the reserve authorities to decide what measures to take when an animal is sick or injured. Cheetahs are an endangered species and the management are not going to allow one of them to die or suffer unnecessarily: as we saw in Chapter 2, they had intervened several years earlier when Amber and her siblings were orphaned, providing them with kills until they were able to hunt for themselves.

All of us who were involved with *Big Cat* were devastated by Honey's death; she was such an amazing character and a wonderful mother. Fortunately her three cubs, who were ten months old at the time, survived, thanks to the efforts of Brian Heath, head of the management team in the Triangle, the special patrol vehicle Cheetah One and the Mara Conservancy rangers, who kept a close eye on them and ensured that they got sufficient food to see them through. Honey's Boys, as we called them, would have stayed with their mother for perhaps another eight months had she lived, so they were a long way from independence. They briefly attached themselves to another cheetah mother with two younger cubs, but by now they were catching smaller prey for themselves, and with the help of 'kills' made for them by the rangers it wasn't long before they were able to fend for themselves, taking up residence on the other side of the river.

Shakira at the den site close to where she gave birth, in the heart of Marsh Lion territory.

Left and opposite:
Jackson Ole Looseyia and
Kate Silverton, the new
faces of *Big Cat Live*.

**D**espite the fact that *Big Cat* had built up
a real following with the general public
over the years, some people felt that it could
do with a bit of a revamp, that it had run its
course or at best needed a makeover. The
talk was of taking it 'live'. This idea had
come about due to the success of live outside
broadcasts in the UK such as *Springwatch*
and *Autumnwatch*, which Simon had co-
presented with Bill Oddie and Kate Humble.
These had gone out on BBC2, but BBC1
were keen to have their own live event and
the commissioners asked if *Big Cat* could
go live. Our series producer Nigel Pope
and the team immediately saw the potential
of this format for us. But the commissioners
and controllers were worried about the
logistics of filming live in Africa and it took
years of cajoling and persuading before
*Big Cat Live* was given the green light.

While Saba was pregnant and decided to
take a break from the programme, one of the
innovations everyone was keen on was to
feature a black Kenyan in a substantial role
as a presenter. Nigel made this his personal
quest. There were a number of drivers and
guides whose knowledge of the Mara and its
wildlife was outstanding. The challenge was
to find someone whose English was easy on
the ear and who had the ability to make the
transition to prime-time television, who had
presence and could articulate their thoughts

on screen. All of us who had met Jackson Ole Looseyia had been impressed with his guiding ability and his communication skills, and he was charming and charismatic too.

Nigel had been working behind the scenes with Jackson, nurturing his talent but being careful not to stifle his natural enthusiasm and unique view of wildlife. They recorded some demos – short informal films on Jackson's areas of interest: everything from a local Masai primary school to the Wildlife Guiding School which Jackson had helped to found with Ron Beaton. The *pièce de résistance* was a film of Jackson flying low across the Mara's dappled plains in a hot-air balloon, his rich, poetic voice adding a lyrical narrative to spectacular scenes of the wildebeest migration. One of the great bonuses of having Jackson on board was that we could address some of the conservation issues relevant to the reserve and introduce the fact that the area owed much of its fame as a wildlife sanctuary to the Masai community whose land it is.

The other new face was Kate Silverton, a co-host of BBC1's breakfast programme, which is a live form of communication requiring a sharp mind, nerves of steel and a confidence in your ability to keep a clear head whatever happens. Kate had cut her teeth as a journalist and proved more than equal to the task of sharing the *Big Cat Live* 'anchor' role with Simon.

**Above:** Kate has years of television experience as a journalist and newsreader and was the ideal choice to anchor the live show - her enthusiasm was infectious and a great boost to the team.

**Above right:** Olive's son Kali - Bella's grandson - at nine months. He promises to be as much a character as his uncle Chui.

**Opposite:** One of Shakira's daughters playing hide and seek under my vehicle. Cheetah cubs become used to the presence of vehicles from the earliest age - hence their relaxed attitude to jumping up onto them later in life.

Going live meant big changes for *Big Cat*. The most obvious was having to film at night if we wished to broadcast in a prime-time slot (the UK is three hours behind Kenya, so 8 o'clock there meant 11 o'clock for us), with the presenters assembling back at camp each night for transmission. Nigel hoped to recreate as much as possible the feeling of being on safari, with the traditional campfire as the heart of the set, just as it had been at *Big Cat* Camp in the past. Simon would operate from 'lion central' – a Land Rover equipped with a bank of TV monitors enabling him to review the live images coming in from the field and to talk to the camera operators. Simon has years of live experience; nothing seems to faze him and he put in a masterly performance.

Nigel also wanted to ring the changes during the live broadcasts by creating a 'secret place' – the snug, as he called it – where two people could

be chatting in a more intimate setting. This worked perfectly when Kate was asking Jackson about his life and experiences, or when she wanted to talk to me about Shakira the cheetah, whose story I was following. For this set Nigel and the floor managers decided on two massive logs colourfully draped with Masai shukas, squares of red patterned cloth. A safari tent with comfortable camp beds and canvas chairs gave an authentic feel. But what made the whole thing come alive was the lighting, imparting an eerie, star-like glow to the surrounding forest, combined with the cinematic effect created by the use of a jib or crane which allowed the camera to swoop down out of the sky. It was as if a space ship was landing in the heart of Planet Africa and winging the images back to our audience in the UK.

We were understandably anxious about just how much usable footage we would be able to record at night. Our old friends the Marsh Lions would be crucial to this, as cheetahs hunt mainly by day and past experience told us that leopards simply could not be relied on to provide more than an occasional glimpse of their beautiful presence. So it was up to the lions to perform. But lions spend an awful lot of time slumped together in a tawny huddle. The ten-day pre-shoot prior to full rehearsal would determine just what we were up against, and I well remember our outside broadcast director David Weir confiding to me how much he loved the Mara in daylight, because to the human eye its beauty lay in the rich tapestry of colours reflected by the blue of the sky, the green of the grassy plains and the earth tones of the acacia woodlands and riverine forest. Such scenes captured in monochrome were only half the picture.

Fortunately the night crew managed to confound all our expectations. Pivotal was Andrew Karanja, who had proved his worth on the very first *Big Cat Diary*. Twelve years ago he had driven the night crew around in much more difficult circumstances while following the Big Pride over rock-strewn terrain more akin to a lunar landscape. For *Big Cat Live* local wildlife artist and stills photographer Peter Blackwell drove the other night vehicle, with Mark MacEwen and Pete McCowen as our night cameramen, each equipped with an infra-red camera and two Ikigami cameras with expensive Canon J40 lenses. Then there was the thermal-imaging camera operated by Luke Barnett, which could see all the way to the horizon, making it indispensable as a spotting scope and in helping to track the lions as they moved about in the darkness. A bonus was that it delivered psychedelic colours straight out of a 1960s hippy party and enabled us to look at the distribution of heat over the bodies of the animals we were filming, clearly illustrating for example how an elephant's ears help it to keep cool by bringing blood close to the surface.

**Stars of Big Cat Diary**

**Masailand**
Wildlife has always been able to thrive among the Masai, who traditionally rely on cattle for most of their needs. Unless a predator takes to killing livestock, the Masai will generally leave it alone.

Kali with a ten-week-old cub. A lioness will charge a person on foot if she feels threatened or that her cubs are at risk.

When there was a full moon – and there was one as we began our live transmissions – it made life very difficult for our night crew, creating just enough light for the prey species to see the predators, which make it much harder for them to hunt. The lions and leopards often responded by steadfastly refusing to waste energy in stalking or ambushing their prey on moonlit nights, though coursing predators such as hyenas and wild dogs, and long-distance sprinters such as cheetahs, were more obliging, quite often hunting when the moon and stars were out. One of the revelations was watching Honey's Boys taking a zebra foal at night. As we had predicted they could now roam wherever they pleased, dominating a large territory all the way south from Musiara Marsh to Paradise Plain and east to Rekero Camp and beyond. They acted as if they owned the place, confidently marking their territory with their individual and collective scent, and checking on any cheetah females they came across – including Shakira – to determine when they might be ready to mate.

The logistics of broadcasting live were mind-boggling. The signal from the remote cameras had to be forwarded via a mid-point – a vehicle situated up on Rhino Ridge in line of sight of Governor's Camp. Our link to the outside world was via a dish that beamed the signal to overhead satellites. To make this happen you first phoned the owner of the satellite and reserved a time allocation for the broadcast. Locating the satellite meant calculating the correct triangulation point by swinging the aerial. The main satellite dish allowed us to transmit to the BBC, with another V satellite dish dedicated to the website. A lot of the equipment had to come from Beijing, where it had been used for the Olympics a month earlier.

Ian Dewar, our engineering manager, recruited from *Springwatch*, was responsible for everything technical on set: lighting, cameras, laying of miles of cable, and the end quality of the images. Key to this was a reliable power source: a custom-built generator and back-up with its own lorry rig which was being shipped from the UK. But to everyone's horror the generator took off on its own mysterious journey around the African continent, settling at one point off the coast of Angola. Despite many phone calls to people of influence the generator failed to arrive in time for the live programmes, let alone the rehearsals scheduled ten days ahead of transmission. Two replacement generators were found in Nairobi, though both were soon struggling to handle the heavy load required to power the whole production. Undeterred, the BBC engineers rebuilt them on site. The missing generator became the talking point of the production, a barometer of our collective optimism that whatever fate might throw at us it would all be all right on the night. Each day storm clouds gathered over camp and we wondered whether the short rains would arrive with a vengeance and provide a test of everyone's planning and resolve. To add to the fun the hyenas trashed the remote cameras and chewed through the cables, but that was only to be expected. Umbrellas appeared briefly during rehearsals but in the end good fortune shined on us and we broadcast live each evening for eight days without a hitch.

One of the most exciting elements of *Big Cat Live* was our dedicated website. Over the past few years Penny Hunter had invested a lot of time and energy in developing the online element of *Big Cat* with a limited budget. This year funding was sufficient to do justice to the multi-platform approach that the BBC hoped *Big Cat Live* would deliver. In just three days the website had overtaken the benchmark established by *Springwatch*, and by the end of transmission had doubled that figure. Particularly popular were the webcams, strategically placed remote cameras offering 24-hour surveillance of three different locations – plains, river and a bird feeder. Viewers could dip

*A rare chance to relax amid the hectic schedule*

in and out of these sites at any time of day online, in the hope that something remarkable might be happening live with our hippos, jackals and hyenas.

Jackson soon became totally engaged with the online operation, providing a live commentary which people loved. Even though the webcams were switched off once we had finished broadcasting, the home page remained on view and 50 short films created especially for the web were uploaded: ground hornbills, an elephant update from the David Sheldrick Wildlife Trust, more on the leopards that Jackson had been following and much else besides. It made *Big Cat Live* totally inclusive, as Penny and her team made

sure that every element of production had a face and a voice.

Whatever we managed to shoot on the day of broadcast had to be edited and packaged within hours so that the presenters could track the story development and script their commentary to fit the footage live on the night. Scott Alexander had the task of keeping abreast of what was going on in the lives of the lions and cheetahs and any other business that was going to be featured that day. As soon as he got up he would establish radio contact with each team in the field to find out what significant events had happened overnight or since they started filming that morning. This allowed him to block out the

running order for that day's programme.

It soon became apparent that Shakira and her cubs were going to be the lead story; and that Honey's Boys would feature strongly too. Shakira's five tiny cubs were simply irresistible, promising all the elements we knew our audience loved best – strong storylines and a personal engagement in the lives of the cats. In the course of the series we were able to dip in and out of the cheetahs' activities and to build a real sense of anticipation. In the end only three of the cubs, all females, survived and we were left wondering what would happen to them on their precarious journey towards independence.

But down on Paradise Plain another drama was unfolding involving one of our previous lion stars. In June 2007 Notch had been ousted from the Marsh Pride by three new males, and his two-year-old relatives – mostly males – had been forced out at the same time. The old male had managed to remain in contact with these youngsters – they were his meal ticket, just as years earlier Scar had lived off the kills made by the adolescent Marsh Lions. Life was repeating itself. Meanwhile Tamu and her two surviving cubs – both males – had tagged along with Notch and the youngsters too. Now Notch had settled on Paradise Plain with his sons and nephews, who at three to four years of age were magnificent young lions, big and powerful with handsome blonde manes. The old male was still instantly recognisable due to the notch in his nostril that had earned him his name, and his magnificent black mane. There was no finer lion in the whole of the Mara. Seeing so many males moving together is rare indeed, and the group roamed both sides of the river, killing hippos. buffaloes and giraffes and mating with a party of young lionesses who would provide them with the nucleus of a new pride.

Because leopards had proved difficult in recent years, and for the third year running Bella had no young cubs, it had been decided that we could not rely on a strong leopard story. Jackson and our ace leopard spotter Paul Karui did manage to track down Bella, who by now was looking very old and weary and had picked up a potentially life-threatening injury when horned by a Thomson's gazelle. Her daughter Olive, however, was proving a star in her own right, having produced two generation of cubs – two females called Binty and Ayah who were about a year-and-a-half old, and a male called Kali who was around seven months and quite a character. Jackson referred to this extended family as the Jackson Five and they helped ensure that leopards remained an important element of *Big Cat*.

Our editors tucked themselves away in the Butterfly House, as it was known, at the edge of

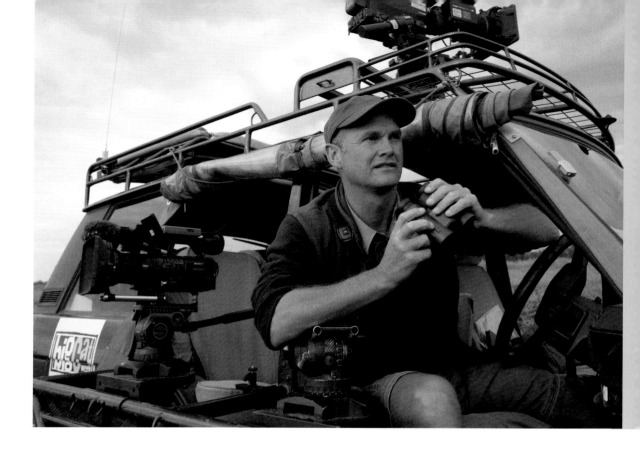

Simon has spent his whole life watching wildlife and is an exceptional naturalist with a deep love of wild places.

the rolling plains surrounding camp, with fans droning all day long to keep the temperature down. The editors' task was to turn around multiple video inserts for the live programmes – 15 to 20 minutes of pre-recorded footage per one-hour programme – to run alongside anything live shown on the night: live footage was always the priority. By 2 pm each day David Weir locked off the running order for that night's show – the inventory of what was going to be shown, where the various pieces of videotape would sit and the balance of the content.

Key to the whole process was Kate's contribution as links presenter. She was on open talkback through her earpiece, receiving a constant wave of communication and direction from David Weir, Nigel Pope and our other series producer Colin Jackson to keep the programme on track regardless of what gremlins might intrude on the night. Kate needed to have total control of the direction the programme was taking, with a

definitive list of cues – up to 50 or 60 per show: these were the threads that held the whole thing together. This meant that she and David had to co-ordinate the first and last words spoken on each piece of video insert, and these were often scripted during early dinner. Simon had an almost equally taxing role at 'lion central', co-ordinating the live lion footage. At the same time all the presenters would be working with the editors right up to transmission, viewing the latest versions of the videotape inserts that we needed to voice live on the show.

At 7 pm we would get miked up and test the talkback through our earpieces to make sure we could hear the voice of whoever was giving us instructions and counting us in and out of each sequence. Around 8 o'clock we would have a full rehearsal – something that I felt might take the edge off the live shows, but that proved a blessing, allowed us to review each piece of videotape

Notch is a true survivor. Since losing his territory he has joined forces with some younger male relatives; together they dominate the lion territories on both sides of the Mara River. Long live the King.

and see how well our commentary complemented the pictures. By the time the titles rolled and the music soared at 11 o'clock we all felt a heightened excitement and energy that helped us to do justice to both the content and our audience.

Nigel and Colin, who alternated as producers for each night's show, would stand watch in the Gallery – a tent with a bank of monitors where David performed his magic, cutting together the images coming in live from the night crew and those streaming in from the remote cameras at the jackal and hyena dens; he would then blend this with the cheetah story and the pieces of pre-recorded videotape. It was a bit like flying a plane. Some sequences overran, forcing the producers to drop videotape inserts that they had planned to show and that we had practised in rehearsal. This accidentally gave a real edge to all our performances, as we could never be sure what might happen next.

A Masai warrior will still face a full-grown male lion, armed only with a spear

167

**Above:** Binty, Olive's two-year-old daughter, leaping effortlessly across the Talek River. In a year or two Binty will have cubs of her own and Bella's legacy will continue in one of the most beautiful parts of the Mara.

**Opposite left:** Two of Kike's cubs clamber onto the roof of Angie's vehicle, investigating the place where their mother has left her mark.

**Opposite right:** Generations of Marsh Lions have inhabited this territory, which looks just as it did when I first came to live here more than 30 years ago. Long may it continue.

At the end of each live programme we breathed a collective sigh of relief, then all the presenters gathered around the campfire for a ten-minute live broadcast over the internet. *Big Cat Raw*, as it was known, provided us with a way of letting off steam after the adrenalin rush of the main programme, and everyone enjoyed the chance to relax and bring a different kind of experience to our web audience. There was a light-heartedness and humour to *Big Cat Raw* that we couldn't risk in the live broadcast – now we could let our hair down a little as Kate fielded a handful of email questions from our audience that formed the basis of our conversations.

One measure of a programme's appeal is the AI (appreciation index) rating it scores, which in our case ranged from 85 to 89. Anything over 80 is considered very good for prime-time factual programming, so there was no question that the *Big Cat* brand was still a potent force and managed to entertain at the highest level throughout. One night we even nudged ITV's *Who Wants to Be a Millionaire* into second place!

We were all in agreement about one thing –

and I found ourselves pinned down in our tent at first light by a family of hungry elephants who had kept everyone in the vicinity awake most of the night as they greedily stripped branches from the trees around the tents. A full complement of armed guards patrolled day and night and everyone was instructed not to move around camp unaccompanied.

Despite everything, the penultimate programme really 'rocked'. The Marsh Pride finally came good with Red stalking a topi just before we went live, then the pride being faced down by a male hippo who dared them to attack him at their peril. Finally there was a glorious segment where the whole pride gambolled about, with cubs and adults putting on a joyous and exuberant play-fest that was just what the audience had been hoping for. It felt more like a 30-minute show than an hour – it whizzed by and when it ended and we went live to the internet *Big Cat Raw* ran for 22 minutes rather than the usual ten. The camera crew was doubled up with laughter, and we all knew that tonight at least we had delivered. The following evening we were relieved just to see the final titles roll without the heavens opening, as they had promised to do virtually every night.

Right at the end of transmission the missing generators with all the lights finally arrived at Mombasa. In their own way they had come to represent the fact that nothing was going to stop *Big Cat Live* from being the success it deserved – rewarding the boldness of those who had always believed that it was possible.

this was the best motivated and energy-charged team that any of us had worked with. We had had plenty of help in making this possible: the senior warden, James Sindiyo, gave us special permission to follow the Marsh Lions at night; and ex-SAS officer Jed Williams, a full-time medic, gave a great sense of reassurance to the whole crew, administering to people with the inevitable stomach upsets, tending to Kate one evening when she tripped and hurt her already tender back and calf muscle just minutes before going live, tutoring Angie and me on basic first aid and assuring one

of the technicians who had been bitten by a large beetle that it was nothing more than a painful nip from the insect's ferocious-looking mouthparts. Everyone was given a safety briefing, always an essential precaution: buffaloes, hippos and elephants are a constant presence around camp and potentially an accident waiting to happen, however experienced you are. Our camp manager, a highly competent professional hunter, was nearly flattened by a bull hippo that charged without warning one night, forcing him to take refuge behind a wire container; and one morning Angie

It is a remarkable tribute to **Big Cat Diary** that it managed to evolve and to sustain people's interest for so long.

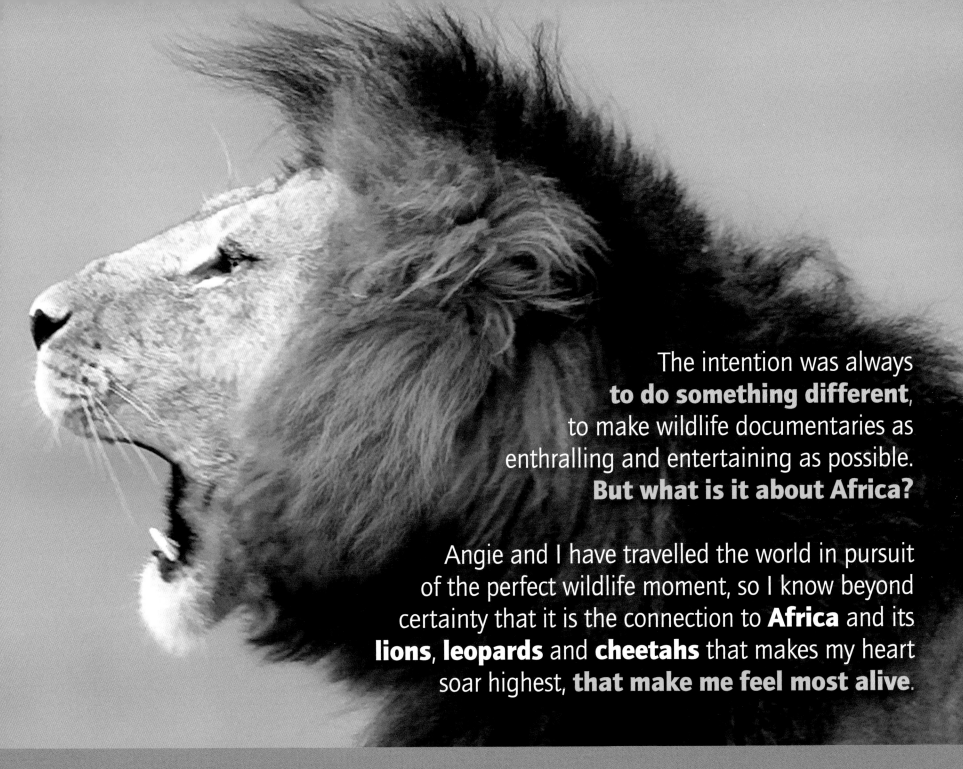

The intention was always **to do something different**, to make wildlife documentaries as enthralling and entertaining as possible. **But what is it about Africa?**

Angie and I have travelled the world in pursuit of the perfect wildlife moment, so I know beyond certainty that it is the connection to **Africa** and its **lions**, **leopards** and **cheetahs** that makes my heart soar highest, **that make me feel most alive**.

George Schaller, renowned zoologist and conservationist, who studied predators in the Serengeti in the 1960s, captured the ambiguous nature of man's relationship with predators in his book *Serengeti: A Kingdom of Predators:*

'Exalted and denigrated, admired and despised, no animals have so aroused the emotions of man as have the large predators...while man fears the predators, he secretly exults in their power, he feels a contagion, an emotional kinship to them. It is no coincidence that visitors to the African parks watch not the impala and zebra, but the lion and leopard... Our dual past still haunts us. We hear a lion roar and the primate in us shivers; we see huge herds of game and the predator in us is delighted, as if our existence still depended on their presence.'

Opposite: One of Honey's cubs in June 2005, nearing the age of independence. Soon he will be old enough to breed and another *Big Cat* dynasty will continue.

Over the years *Big Cat* has managed to capture many of these emotions. In 2005 we recorded a one-hour special called *Big Cat Diary: The Big Story*, a celebration of ten years of the series. The highlights were moments of intense drama such as when the buffaloes wreaked havoc along the Bila Shaka Lugga, killing one of the Marsh Pride's cubs, and when the male lion threatened Honey and her three cubs over in the Mara Triangle. And who could forget Toto's lucky escape from the baboons? We were reminded of times spent in the company of Half-Tail and Zawadi, and more recently Bella, whom Saba had the privilege of watching with two young cubs; there was Simon's relationship with Notch the king of lions and Honey the queen of cheetahs; and Kike, who came to think of my car as a convenient aerial latrine.

For *The Big Story*, each of the presenters summed up their feelings about working on *Big Cat*. Saba had this to say: 'You have a unique situation here which is that for the last ten years the BBC has been filming known cats and then family dynasties and that's something normally a very few selected handful of scientists have the privilege of being able to do. It's part entertainment but on the other side it has real value, which is making people care about the animals and hopefully helping to conserve them in the long run.' Simon echoed this: 'The important conservation message is inherent in the amount of care, attention and emotional investment that we, and I believe the audience, have given to the individual creatures that we followed – I hope so.'

As for me, I said that one of the things I am most proud of is 'when people come up to me when we drive around and say, "You know why we're here? We're here because of *Big Cat Diary* – we heard about the Masai Mara through your TV programmes, we wanted to visit and see that for ourselves." That means we're helping to protect the wildlife because the revenue from tourism is so important to countries like Kenya in maintaining areas such as this and keeping them free, keeping them wild.'

Thirty-five years ago I saw my first wild lions in the Serengeti. I stayed on in Africa to pursue my love of wild creatures, and in many ways what you see on *Big Cat Diary* mirrors what Angie and I do for a living. Time and again we return to Musiara Marsh, Paradise Plain, Leopard Gorge and the Talek River, keeping track of what is happening in the lives of the big cats we have come to know so intimately. As I said in *The Big Story*: 'I've grown old with *Big Cat Diary*. You know, ten years – that's a long time not just in television, that's a long time in your life. For as long as I can I'm going to be here in the Masai Mara telling the story of these cats.' And that is the beauty of *Big Cat*. Though it is indeed a soap opera of sorts, it was never anything but real life. There was nothing contrived, just the raw beauty of nature delivered right into your living rooms, and if you choose to you can journey to the Mara yourselves and experience that reality first hand. The big cats are a reminder of man's animal past and, for the moment at least, in protected areas their lives continue undiminished by what is happening in our world – and whether or not we are there recording theirs.

Just before completing this book I went down to the Mara to appear in the final episode in a new reality series called *To the Ends of the Earth*. This was another step

forward in exploring the possibilities of making natural history ever more current, a partnership between the BBC Natural History Unit and BBC Entertainment (who make hugely popular family viewing such as *Strictly Come Dancing*). For the contestants, what was on offer was the opportunity to win a year's placement as a cameraperson with the NHU – an ideal apprenticeship for anyone hoping to become a wildlife film-maker. Nine people were chosen from thousands of applicants with the criteria being a passion for natural history as much as any film-making skills or prior experience. Over the course of eight weeks these nine contestants were taken to some of Africa's most cherished wildlife destinations until the number had been whittled down to three. Each new location was kept a secret,

so you can imagine how excited the finalists were to find themselves on safari in *Big Cat* country, with the production team located in the *Big Cat* Camp and the contestants a few hundred metres upstream on the banks of the Mara River.

It was just like old times and the ideal opportunity for me to catch up on the stars of *Big Cat Live*. Shakira and her three daughters were a delight to watch as they scampered around the vehicles and thickets, with Shakira as alert as ever to danger, though at eight months the youngsters had a good chance of surviving to maturity. We also saw Honey's Boys, who looked in the peak of condition. For me the joy of watching these three males was in knowing their history, in having witnessed their lives from cubhood to the present. Their existence was

a tribute to Honey's skills as a mother.

A month or so earlier Angie and I had hosted a photo-workshop with Warren Samuels at Rekero Camp along the Talek River, where Jackson Ole Looseyia is based. Jackson and his team were able to help us find some of the Jackson Five, though there was no sign of Bella. But we saw Olive on a number of occasions with her son Kali – Chui's nephew, now a year old. We also saw Binty, Olive's daughter, now nearing independence, wandering along a beautiful stretch of the Talek. At one point she gathered herself and leapt high in the air, her tail outstretched, as she forded the river. Then she just melted away into the thickets and was gone.

While the leopard stuns the senses with its beauty, the cheetah catches your breath with its feline grace and athleticism – its blinding burst of speed. But it is the lion that we stand in awe of. So it was to Paradise Plain that I travelled in the hope of one last look at Notch, the old Marsh Pride male who, with his five – sometimes six, people say – younger male relatives, was causing quite a stir in this part of the Mara. During *Big Cat Live* Angie had managed to keep track of Notch for much of the time and each night she would regale me with stories about him and his companions. Imagine seeing so many male lions travelling together, watching as the younger among them paid their respects to Notch. At one point Notch and one of these youngsters stood face to face, thumb-sized canines bared, testing each other's nerve and courage. You could feel the tension, see the outline of their breath in the early morning cold as the younger male eventually reluctantly turned aside. All of us knew that in Angie's photos we were witnessing both the rise and eventual fall of a king among predators.

While Angie is a Kenya Citizen I am not, so I would like to thank the Kenya government for allowing me to live and work in their amazing country, which I am honoured to call my home. The Masai Mara National Game Reserve, where Big Cat is filmed, falls within two districts, one run by the Narok County Council (NCC), the other managed by the Mara Conservancy. The wardens of these two areas have always been very generous and supportive of our work. In this respect we would particularly like to thank Senior Wardens Michael Koikai, James Sindiyo and Stephen Minis from NCC, and Senior Warden David Seur, Brian Heath and Jonny Baxendale from the Mara Triangle.

All photos by Angela and Jonathan Scott except.... Page 71: Baby olive baboon by David Scott. Page 90: Bella and cub silhouette by Ian Johnson. Page 126: Andy Chastney and wart hog by Mandy Knight.

We owe a special vote of thanks to my fellow presenters Simon King and Saba Douglas-Hamilton for agreeing to collaborate with us on this book, and to Kate Silverton and Jackson Ole Looseyia, who joined us on *Big Cat Live* and contributed star performances of their own.

It is always a privilege to work with the BBC Natural History Unit, who make the best wildlife documentaries in the world. Keith Scholey, whose vision helped create *Big Cat Diary*, has been hugely supportive of our efforts, as have former heads of the NHU Alastair Fothergill and Neil Nightingale. The sheer energy of our executive producer Sara Ford never failed to give everyone a boost when she visited the Mara, while series producers Nigel Pope and Colin Jackson played a significant role in ensuring everything ran smoothly at the *Big Cat* Camp. Nigel has been particularly helpful in providing us with details of just what it took to take *Big Cat* 'live'. Robin Hellier was another stalwart as series and then executive producer.

Executive producer Fiona Pitcher oversaw the transition of the series back to BBC1 in 2003 as *Big Cat Week* and nurtured Saba's arrival as our third presenter. We are grateful also to series producers Wendy Darke, Stephen Moss, Richard Matthews and Miles Barton; production co-ordinators Mandy Knight and Jenni Collie at *Big Cat* Camp; production manager Lynn Barry in Bristol; sound engineer Andy Milk, who was the person to know whenever there was a technical problem; Willy Gitai in the vehicle department; and Jean Hartley and her team at Viewfinders in Nairobi. Life in the bush is only possible with this kind of support.

It is impossible to list everyone who has been involved with *Big Cat* over the years but key characters not already mentioned include:

Camera: Gavin Thurston, Richard Matthews, Richard North, Toby Strong, Warwick Sloss, Gordon Buchanan, Warren Samuels, John Aitchison, Pete McCowen, Martyn Colbeck, Mark Yates, Richard Ganicliff, Hugh Maynard, Andy McClennahan, Mike Fox, Hitesh Makan, Simon Bell, Richard Slater-Jones, Michael Kelem and Barbara Tyack

Field team: David and Natasha Breed, Peter Blackwell, Lisa Asch, William Kipen, Wilson Wemali, Sammy Munene, Aidan Woodward, Paul Kirui, Ian Johnson, Chris Brennan, Andrew Karanja, David Scott and Dave Sexton

Producers: Marguerite Smits van Oyen, Lizzie Bewick, Lucy Meadows, Matt Thompson, Roger Webb, Hugh Pearson, Adam Chapman, Duncan Chard, Huw Cordey, James Brickell, Ben Aviss and Kate Hubert

Editors: Andrew Chastney, Steve White, Deborah Williams, Nick Carline, Melissa Warren, Ivan Jones, Steve Phillips, Dan Clamp and Andy Derbyshire

Sound recordists: Andy Hawley, Dave Parkinson, Chris Watson, Dickie Bird, Chris Taylor and Mike Burgess

Production managers/co-ordinators: Lisanne O'Keefe, Kirsty Reid, Zoe Kerr, Nikki Andrews, Helen Williams, Helen Healey, Ellie Williams, Siobhan Brook and Jolie Bradfield

Website: Penny Hunter

Music: David Poore

Camera vehicle: Phineas Kangi and Stanley Kinyolo

The Grammaticus family at Musiara Ltd who own the Governor's group of camps outfitted the *Big Cat* Camp – as did our old friend Jock Anderson of East African Wildlife Safaris in earlier days. Governor's have always been generous in providing Angie and me with a base in the Mara. And we simply couldn't have kept on the road without Patrick Beresford and his team at the Governor's Camp workshop. Thanks are also due to Collin Wellensky (and his vegetable garden), Dave Richards and Annick Mitchell at Governor's and Patrick Reynolds at Il Murran. Stephen Mutua, formerly head driver and now naturalist at Governor's Camp, has been a friend for many years and was a mine of information on what our big cats were doing in our absence. All the driver-guides at Governor's were immensely helpful and many of them worked as spotters for *Big Cat Diary*: Emmanuel Kantai, John Amugune, Solomon Kenduiywo, Dickson Ntalengo, Phipip Nzuve, Fed Kinaiyia, Francis

Sadera, Samuel Ruto, Jacob Lelesara, Robert Chebusit, Joseph Mandila, Moses Manduku, Josephat Kamandole, Stephen Karani, Japhet Kivango, Gideon Kuluo, Stephen Wakubwa, Stanley Koech, Simon Sitienei, Jacob Ngunjiri, Isack Langat, Fancisco Ntuala, Joash Moturi, Simon Maroro, Anthony Mbithi, Joseph Mwangi, Juma Saidi, Francis Ndongo, Wilson Towet, Charles Kerore, Wilson Lolapit, Julius Olenana, and David Mbusia – a huge vote of thanks to you all.

Caroline Taggart has been our editor for 30 years and we cannot thank her enough. Jonny Pegg worked miracles as our literary agent, unerringly patient and intuitive when problems arose. Darren Westlake at TU ink is a gem of a designer. We wanted this book to look different, boasting a more modern feel while still doing justice to the magnificence of our star big cats: the proof is in the finished product, a book we can all be proud of. There would have been no book at all if it hadn't been for Harry Ricketts, who published a previous title of ours, *Mara-Serengeti: A Photographer's Paradise*, and who introduced us to Lord Evans and Caroline Smith of Evans Mitchell Publishers, who maintained faith in this project under difficult circumstances and spared no cost in ensuring a beautiful book. Publicist Sally Woodyatt of Polka Dot PR worked tirelessly to gain maximum publicity. Daniel Mirzoeff of the BBC Commercial Agency

acted on all matters concerning rights. Tim Harris and Lee Dalton at NHPA/Photoshot picture agency were generous with their time whenever we needed to access our wildlife images.

Angie's brother David Bellamy and his wife Mishi have always been there for us when we needed them, as have my sister Caroline and brother Clive and his wife Judith. Our children Alia and David and David's wife Tara are our inspiration. A number of friends in the UK have provided us with a home from home over the years, particularly Cissy and David Walker, Pam Savage and Michael Skinner, Pippa and Iain Stewart-Hunter, Brian and Annabelle Jackman, Dr Michael and Sue Budden, Charles and Lindsay Dewhurst, Paul and Donna Goldstein, Peter and Jennie Hughes, Keith and Liz Scholey, Robin and Elin Hellier, Peter and Grace Mason, Paul and Carole Nicholson, Mark Carwardine, Kim and Nicky Gotlieb, and Kelvin and Simone Lack. Their generosity is beyond the call of duty.

In America Carole Wyman has been a wonderful friend to our whole family, and in Kenya our good neighbours Frank and Dolcie Howitt continue to keep an eye on us with unerring generosity. Fellow photographer Nigel Pavitt was always there for us in our hour of need for technical support. Barry van Vuuren and Valerie Roth-Bousquet at Canon Europa in Holland were immensely generous, as were Chris Elworthy of Red Dot and formerly Canon Camera Division (UK), and Brian Hall of Experience Seminars. John Brinkley, Peter Antoniou and Christine Percy at Swarovski Optik (UK) have been great supporters too.

*Angie and I are blessed to live the life of our dreams, but we never forget that we simply couldn't do this without an awful lot of help. Thank you all.*